STUDYING FOR PSYCHOLOGY

STUDYING FOR PSYCHOLOGY

DONNA L. MEALEY
Louisiana State University

WILLIAM D. MCINTOSH
Georgia Southern University

BRENDA D. SMITH, Series Editor
Georgia State University

HarperCollins*CollegePublishers*

Acquisitions Editor: Ellen Schatz
Cover Designer: Ruttle Graphics, Inc./D. Setser
Electronic Production Manager: Angel Gonzalez Jr.
Publishing Services: Ruttle Graphics, Inc.
Electronic Page Makeup: Ruttle Graphics, Inc.
Printer and Binder: R. R. Donnelley & Sons Company
Cover Printer: The Lehigh Press, Inc.

Studying for Psychology, First Edition

Library of Congress Cataloging-in-Publication Data

Mealey, Donna L.

Studying for psychology / Donna L. Mealey, William D. McIntosh.

p. cm.

Includes index.

ISBN 0-06-500648-8

1. Psychology—Study and teaching (Higher) I. McIntosh, William D. II. Title

BF77.M38 1995

150'.71'1—dc20 94-12577

CIP

95 96 97 9 8 7 6 5 4 3 2 1

Dedication

To our parents for supporting us through endless years of education.

ACKNOWLEDGMENTS

We would like to acknowledge the help and encouragement of several groups and individuals in the conception, writing, and publication of this book.

First, thank you to our many students at the University of Georgia, Louisiana State University, and Georgia Southern University for guiding us to consider what approaches and assistance would most support their college learning.

We also appreciate those mentors and colleagues at the same universities who taught us a great deal about instruction, students, and writing. Special thanks to Sherrie Nist for the many opportunities she provided to learn about college reading and learning.

Thanks, too, to the reviewers who helpfully critiqued several drafts of the manuscript: Judith Wrase Nygard, Mercer County Community College, Deborah R. Winters, New Mexico State University, Linda K. Davis, Mt. Hood Community College, Nannette Commander, Georgia State University, and F. Kim Wilcox, University of Missouri—Kansas City.

We are grateful to Brenda Smith for including us in this series and for her guidance as the project developed. We also appreciate the assistance of the folks at HarperCollins, specifically Jane Kinney, Marisa L'Heureux, Mark Paluch, and Ellen Schatz, who were there when we needed them and who backed off when we needed them to do that, too.

Finally, we want to thank Larry and Debbie for their patience with our impatience and their unflagging support.

D.L.M.

W.D.M.

TO THE STUDENT

Studying for Psychology is designed to give you a solid grounding in the basics of psychology as well as the basics of studying. As you learn study strategies, you are also learning about Freud, memory, emotions, the brain, child development, and much more.

The first two chapters introduce you to a mindset for both studying and the field of psychology. Chapter 1, "Getting Ready for Psychology," provides you with some hints about getting prepared to study, where to study, how to analyze the syllabus for your psychology course, and how to find motivation for studying psychology, if you have not already done so. Chapter 2, "Psychology: The Big Picture," helps you understand how the field of psychology is organized into seven main areas and suggests ways to figure out how your instructor may think about psychology.

Chapters 3 and 4 introduce you to strategies for reading your psychology textbook and for taking notes in class. In Chapter 3, "Reading Psychology," you will learn how to preview your textbook, brainstorm, and break up reading into manageable assignments. You will also be shown how to use the reading strategy of text annotation and why it has many benefits over merely highlighting text. Chapter 4, "Taking Lecture Notes in Psychology," helps you evaluate your current note taking techniques and introduces you to a technique of long-standing success, the Cornell method.

Chapter 5, "The Language of Psychology," discusses the importance of concepts and vocabulary in psychology and provides you with strategies for figuring out which words to learn and for studying terminology effectively. In addition, Appendix 1 provides you with a listing of important psychological terms to know, explains many of the more complex concepts, and helps you figure out how to learn and remember these concepts.

Chapter 6, "Maximizing Your Memory," explains how memory works, and how the information you learn about memory in your psychology textbook and class can help you become a better student. You will be introduced to several memory-improving strategies, such as imagery, method of loci, and acronyms, as well as to some of the limitations of memory.

In contrast to "shallow" memory strategies, study strategies help you learn material at "deeper" levels. Chapter 7, "Studying Psychology," introduces you to the idea of "active studying" and shows you how to use your text annotations as the basis for constructing study strategy materials, such as maps and charts, timelines, study guides, and vocabulary cards.

Chapter 8, "Preparing for Tests in Psychology," demonstrates strategies for preparing for essay and objective exams. We provide a sample of an essay response, and several sample essay questions keyed to the seven areas of psychology discussed in Chapter 2 are given in Appendix 1. In addition to tips on taking multiple choice tests, Appendix 2 provides a sample of a multiple choice introductory psychology test. All of these samples are provided with the intention of helping you learn to predict possible test questions and prepare effectively for your exams. This chapter also presents a strategy, to be used a night or two before a test, which helps you summarize and think about all the information and concepts on which you will be tested. In addition, this chapter presents techniques for coping with test anxiety both before and during tests.

Finally, Chapter 9, "All the Other Parts of Your Life," discusses some of the findings of psychology that relate to the quality of your life outside your classes. You do not go to classes and study in a vacuum, the rest of your life influences your college career. To do well and be successful in school really requires that you are comfortable in the other aspects of you life. Because this book is about studying and psychology, it seems appropriate to say something about what psychologists know about getting and staying happy.

The key to all of this information is not to leave it in the book. Therefore, we have included application exercises at the end of every chapter to help you connect what you learn to your psychology class. If you effectively use what you learn in this book, you will do better in your psychology class, and you will be a better student in general.

D.L.M.

W.D.M.

CONTENTS

CHAPTER 1

GETTING READY FOR PSYCHOLOGY

GETTING FOCUSED

- *What does psychology study?*
- *How can you organize yourself to study efficiently?*
- *How can you detect important clues to success in your psychology syllabus?*
- *How can you participate in psychology experiments?*
- *How can you motivate yourself to study psychology?*
- *How can you relate psychology to real life?*

The purpose of this book is to introduce you to the study of psychology and to help you get an inside track on achieving success in your introductory psychology course. To meet this purpose, we have tried simultaneously to keep one foot in the field of psychology and the other in the field of studying and learning from text and lecture.

Your time is precious. You already have a great deal of reading to do for your classes. Why should you purchase and read a book on how to study psychology when you could be spending that time reading your psychology text? We can think of six important reasons:

1. If you competently apply what you learn in this book to your work in your psychology course, you are likely to do well.

2. This book presents effective study and learning strategies using examples selected solely from psychology, so it is highly relevant and applicable to your course experience.

3. This book clarifies many confusing psychology concepts.

4. This book offers "inside information" and many hints on important psychology terminology to know, sample test questions and responses, and practical ways to learn and remember psychology concepts and theories.

5. What you learn from this book will help you not only in psychology, but also in your other social science courses.

6. Finally, you can use the book as a reference and read only those sections for which you have an immediate need, or you can use it as a companion to your psychology textbook and read the entire book.

That said, we invite you to plunge into psychology and its study with *both* feet.

PSYCHOLOGY STUDIES US

Sex. (Do we have your attention?) Violence. (How about now?) Addiction. Love. Romance. Happiness. Depression. Jealousy. Aggression. Hunger. Bodies and brains. Reward and punishment. War and peace.

Remembering and forgetting. Talking. Thinking. Mob behavior. Enlightenment. Stress.

These words may sound like descriptions of a TV movie of the week or a steamy novel, but they actually get at the heart of psychology. Although your psychology class and textbook may seem a little more intense and technical than a romance novel, psychology deals with the "stuff" of our lives: how we think, feel, act, change, learn, and grow.

There is very little in psychology that does not relate to your own life in some way. You use memory, fall in love, were a kid once, have a brain, use language, and so on. Most of these topics are already familiar to you. You are just going to explore them in a little more depth and a bit more formally. Try to keep this in mind as you go through your psychology course. The way an idea is presented may be foreign, or the terminology used may seem complicated, but the ideas themselves are not. One of the purposes of this book is to help you navigate through the complex terminology and sometimes foreign manner in which ideas are presented in psychology. *Studying for Psychology* will give you an edge in understanding how familiar you already are with much of psychology as well as in helping to correct misconceptions about psychology that you may have.

A Note of Caution: Don't Ignore the Obvious

One important point to keep in mind from the start, however, is to try not to get *too* comfortable when you come across ideas with which you are already familiar. Some aspects of psychology seem very obvious, and you may tend to ignore this information when you first hear it or read about it.

Do not take for granted that something is obvious and that you'll know it at test time. If you do, you may find that you cannot remember which of the four "very obvious" multiple choice options in front of you is the one you heard in class or read about in your textbook.

One example of taking the obvious for granted are the statements: "opposites attract" and "birds of a feather flock together." If your psychology instructor told you that when it comes to romantic relationships, "opposites attract," you might not be very surprised. After all, most people have heard that phrase many times. It's obvious: People tend to get romantically involved with others who are very different from themselves. What if your instructor told you that when it comes to romantic relationships, "birds of a feather flock together," that people who are similar to each other tend to be attracted to each other? That also sounds rather obvious. So, which is it? Are people more likely to date others who are like them or unlike them? The truth of the matter is that we tend to be attracted to people who are similar to us.[1] We are more likely to date people who are similar to us in interests, attitudes, religious orientation, and family background.

You can see the problem. Sometimes, students fall into the trap of thinking that a lot of material in psychology is too obvious to write down. Often, very obvious things get hazy and confused as time goes by. In addition, when psychology instructors write test questions, they are aware of what seems to be obvious to students, and they are skilled at phrasing questions so that they discriminate between students who learned the material and students who figured it was too obvious to study.

"Confusing" Test Questions

Let's say, for example, that your instructor is describing how psychologists determine when a person is suffering from a mental illness. There are four things to consider about a person's behavior when deciding whether a person is mentally ill:

1. The behavior is atypical; most people would not behave in this way.

2. The behavior is disturbing to others.

3. The behavior is maladaptive. That is, it is hard for the person to lead a normal, happy life when he or she behaves in this way.

4. The behavior is unjustifiable; there is no good reason for the behavior.

---

[1] B. L. Warren, "A Multi-variable Approach to the Assortive Mating Phenomenon," *Eugenics Quarterly*, 13, (1966), 285–298.

All of these considerations make sense and seem obvious enough. Now, on the test, your instructor might ask the following multiple choice question:

Which of the following is NOT one of the four factors taken into consideration when deciding whether a person's behavior indicates that she or he is suffering from a psychological disorder?

a. The behavior is disturbing to others.
b. The behavior is unpredictable.
c. The behavior is maladaptive.
d. The behavior is unjustifiable.
e. The behavior is atypical.

Do you see how it might be difficult to remember which of these choices (choice b) was not mentioned as an indicator of mental illness after a few weeks have gone by since the lecture or reading assignment? When you come across something that you think you will need to know, make a note of it, even if you think you already know it. With this important point about psychology in mind, let's start getting organized.

GETTING SITUATED: WHERE TO STUDY

Before we get to what you are going to study, let's think about where you are going to study. Place is a much more important consideration than you might think. Listen to the story of a reformed slob.

Up until a few years ago, one of the authors did most of his work on a small metal table. His computer took up nearly all the space on the table. Because there was not much room for anything else, he usually had stacks of papers and books all over the edges of the table and on the floor. It never occurred to him to think about the effect that his work space might be having on his work. Often, he would misplace the same piece of paper over and over in the course of a few minutes.

Then, he did something that changed his entire outlook on work. He bought a gigantic desk, so big that the delivery men had to take it apart to get it through the front door. Suddenly, he had all this space, and an incredible thing happened. Not only did it help him organize all of those papers and books, but it actually made it easier to organize his thoughts. He was able to concentrate better and for longer periods of time, as if the clutter around his little table had been cluttering his head as well.

Clean Surroundings, Clearer Mind

Having a clean space designated for studying makes sense when you think about it. When you go for a walk in the woods, your thoughts become calm and clear. When you go for a walk on a city street during rush hour, it is a lot harder to have slow, calm, clear thoughts. Our surroundings have a huge impact on our thoughts, but we rarely notice it.

We are not suggesting that you purchase a gigantic desk to work on, but try to be aware of where you choose to work. Even if you are not particularly neat, make a point of keeping your study area clutter-free.

Notice the phrase *study area* in the last sentence. That phrase was not carelessly chosen. Not only is it important to keep the area where you study nice and clean, it is also important that you have one designated study area where you do nothing but study. Think of it as sacred ground that you would never defile with newspapers, food, TV, or snoring. If you are not going to study, do not go into your study area, except to clean it.

▪

PERSONAL LEARNING QUESTIONS

What does your study space look like? Is it workable? Remove as many distractions as possible: magazines, television, letters, trash, etc. Organize to give yourself a clean desktop and neat bookshelves and desk drawers.

▪

Clean Desks and Classical Conditioning

To explain the importance of keeping your study area for studying only, we have to introduce a psychological concept: **classical conditioning.** Classical conditioning is one basic way that we learn things; even simple animals, like flatworms and wombats, learn through classical conditioning. You may have heard of **Pavlov** and his famous salivating dogs. Pavlov made classical conditioning famous. He found that if you ring a bell right before you give dogs food, and you go through this procedure over and over, eventually the dogs will start salivating in

Learn to associate your study area with one and only one activity: studying.

anticipation of dinner whenever you ring the bell. They will salivate at the sound of the bell even when food is nowhere in sight.[2]

The basic idea of classical conditioning is that we learn to associate things that are repeatedly paired. For example, if you work in a chocolate factory and hate your job, you will eventually learn to hate the smell of chocolate because you associate it with your job. "Yes, but what do dog saliva and chocolate have to do with my study habits?" you ask. If you only study in your study area, you will quickly learn to associate that area with one and only one activity—studying. You will not be easily distracted with thoughts of food or a quick nap, because this area does not conjure up thoughts of these activities. Don't sleep at your desk, don't eat at your desk, don't watch TV at your desk, don't read the newspaper at your desk, and you will concentrate better and

---

[2] I. P. Pavlov, *Conditioned Reflexes,* trans. and ed. G. V. Anrep (New York: Dover, 1960). (Original translation Oxford University Press, 1927.)

get your work done faster. When you are done, you can go somewhere else and devote all of your concentration to eating, sleeping, or watching TV.

GETTING ORIENTED: USE YOUR SYLLABUS AS A MAP

Now that you have a sacred study area for the semester, let's take a look at what your psychology course holds in store for you. The course syllabus is a good place to start because it often provides some hints about what your instructor thinks is important to know. You can think of the syllabus as a map that will guide you through the semester: it often has directions, and it charts a route for you to follow. The syllabus can help you get oriented because it should contain important information that can help you do well in the course, such as descriptions of the kinds of tests or papers that will be required, test dates, the amount of time spent on each topic, grading, attendance policies, and purposes of the course. You can also learn a lot from seeing what it does not mention, such as chapters that you do not have to read.

Obviously, each instructor's syllabus contains different information and assignments, but you should find most of the information that we discuss. The sample course syllabus in Table 1.1 on pages 10–11 will illustrate the important information you need to know. Make sure you at least have all the information mentioned in Table 1.2 on page 14, "What to Look for in the Syllabus."

What's Important in the Syllabus?

First, use the syllabus from your psychology course to examine the basics.

1. Who is the instructor?

   ____

   Some students go through an entire quarter or semester not knowing who their instructor is because they did not care to remember or because they missed the first day of class. Knowing who your instructor is gives you that first important connection to him or her. If you attach a name to the face, you may feel more comfortable going to see the instructor during office hours when you have questions. Although you've probably often heard this piece of advice, it's true that making yourself known amongst a sea of unknown faces in a large lecture hall rarely hurts you and can often help you.

2. Where is the instructor's office?

 ____

3. When are office hours held?

 ____

4. What is the office phone number?

 ____

 If this information is not provided, ask the instructor to fill in the blanks. As a paying student, you are entitled to know how to contact your instructor for help.

5. What textbook is required? Is more than one listed?

 ____

 ____

 Usually, an introductory psychology course requires one large text and, possibly, a study guide. Make sure you buy the *right* textbook. Large universities usually run several sections of introductory psychology each semester, and each instructor may use a different textbook. You do not want to have the text for Section 5 if you are enrolled in Section 2.

6. Read the course objectives or course description. This information gives you a glimpse of what the semester will be like, how the instructor expresses herself or himself, and what her or his vision is for the course. It may even tell you point-blank what you are expected to learn.

7. How will your grade be determined?

 ____

 ____

 ____

(continued on page 12)

TABLE 1.1 SAMPLE COURSE SYLLABUS

INTRODUCTION TO PSYCHOLOGY

I. Basic Information

Instructor:	Dr. Bill McIntosh
Office:	Math/Physics/Psy Rm. 116
Office Hrs.	M–F 10:00–11:00 A.M.
Phone:	555–5555
Textbook:	*Introduction to Psychology*
Author:	Robin S. Thompson

II. Course Objectives

The purpose of Introductory Psychology is to introduce you to the field of psychology. We'll be looking at some of the highlights and important findings that have come out of all the various areas of study that make up the field of psychology. If you're a psych major, or are considering being a psych major, this course will form the foundation for all of your later courses. But even if you're not a psych major, Intro Psych can be useful as more than just meeting a requirement. Phil Donahue and Oprah can't seem to get through even one show without having a psychologist commenting on the proceedings, and Coke spends millions of dollars learning how to persuade you to buy their product. An understanding of psychology gives you the ability to understand, evaluate, and make your own choices about the things you encounter that involve psychology.

III. Course Requirements

A. Grading—Your grade will be based on five tests, a final exam, and two written assignments. The tests will be multiple choice. Each test is worth 12% of your grade. The final exam is cumulative and will include both multiple choice and short answer questions. It is worth 30% of your grade. The final 10% of your grade will be based on the written assignments.

B. Reading Assignments—Please keep up with the reading assignments in the text. I won't be constantly reminding you of where you should be in the reading. It's best to stay slightly ahead of the lectures. Each test will include some questions that were covered in the text but not in class, just as it will include some questions that were covered in class but not in the book.

C. Missing Quizzes—If you won't be able to take a test at the scheduled time, please let me know in advance. All makeup tests will be given on the last class day of the quarter. No makeups will be given at any other time under any other circumstances. Under no circumstances will anyone be allowed to make up more than one test. Makeup tests will be short-answer in format.

D. Attendance—There is no formal attendance policy in this class. But if you don't come to class regularly, be warned that people who don't come to this class invariably do not do well.

E. Written Assignments—The purpose of the written assignments is for you to look at how the topics we cover exist in the "real world." The topics will be described at length later in the quarter. Assignments should be typed, proofread, and stapled.

IV. Other Information

Research Participation: All students are required to participate in one psychological experiment as part of the requirements for the course. In addition, you have the opportunity to earn extra credit for participating in more than one experiment. The particulars are given in a separate handout. Please read it carefully.

For each extra study you participate in, you receive 1 percentage point added to your final grade, up to a maximum of 3. Studies are run from early in the quarter through week 9 of classes. No studies are conducted in the final week of classes. Sometimes the sign-up sheets fill up quickly, so get there early if you want to participate.

V. Tentative Course Outline

Topic	*Assignment*	*Topic*	*Assignment*
1. Introduction	Chapter 1	9. Motivation and emotion	Chapter 10
2. Biology and behavior	Chapter 2	• The hierarchy of needs	
3. Sensation and perception	Chapter 3	• Happiness	
4. Consciousness	Chapter 4	10. Personality	Chapter 11
• Waking consciousness		• Freud	
• Dreams		• Humanism	
• Hypnosis		• Trait theory	
• Drugs		11. Psychological disorders	Chapter 12
5. Learning	Chapter 5	• Anxiety	
• Classical & operant conditioning		• Multiple personalities	
6. Memory and cognition	Chapter 6	• Depression	
• How memory works		• Schizophrenia	
• Findings relevant to studying		• Personality disorders	
7. Language and intelligence	Chapter 7	12. Therapy	Chapter 13
• Teaching human language to animals		13. Social psychology	Chapters 14 & 15
• Communication styles of males and females		• Social influence	
8. Development	Chapters 8 & 9	• Aggression and altruism	
		• Love	

8. Note what kind of exams you will have. Are they multiple choice, essay, short answer, or some combination of these?

____

____

We will help you make good use of this information in Chapter 8, which covers test preparation. If this information is not on the syllabus, ask the instructor what kind of tests she or he gives. You have the right to know ahead of time so that you can plan how to study; that is, you may study differently for an essay test than you would for a multiple-choice exam.

9. How many tests will be given and when? How much does each one count towards your final grade?

____

____

____

You need to know right from the start if your grade will be determined by only a midterm and a final, or if you will be tested weekly. This information will help you determine how much time you need to allot each week for studying psychology and the importance of each test in calculating your final grade. Although specific dates may be difficult for an instructor to state at the beginning of the semester, he or she should be able to give you an indication of approximately when tests will be given.

10. Often, an attendance policy is included in the syllabus. This information is important. What does your instructor expect from you? Is attendance taken at every class meeting?

____

Excessive absences may bring down your grade, especially if you are on the borderline between two grades.

11. Are there any other cautions, warnings, or suggestions for success offered? Often, instructors will offer extra credit assignments,

warnings about tardiness, and suggestions for studying in the syllabus. It really pays to read this document very carefully.

12. Take a look at the topics you will be covering. (See V, "Tentative Course Outline," in Table 1.1.) This information tells you how much class time will be spent on each topic and can be helpful when you are devising a study plan for exams. For example, if you are going to spend two weeks on "Learning" and two days on "Social Psychology," your instructor probably thinks the chapter on learning is very important. Thus, you will want to make an extra effort to understand the material on learning.

13. Get an idea of how many chapters you will be required to read and learn, and figure a rough estimate of how many chapters that boils down to per week. This early estimate will give you a good indication of your workload, and you can start planning your semester accordingly.

14. Take a good look at the topics you are going to cover and see which topics are of particular interest to you. As we will discuss shortly, motivation is a key factor in your success in any course. Anticipating interesting material to come will get you energized to get started.

15. As you evaluate the syllabus, remember that you are in effect "purchasing" this course, and you may be able to exchange it for another. Most psychology departments offer more than one section of introductory psychology during any one semester. If your instructor is not going to emphasize topics that you really wanted to learn about, or if you honestly think the work load required by this particular instructor is unreasonable, or if you just plain do not like the instructor, change to another instructor's introductory psychology class, if possible.

Seek out the opinions of students who have previously taken the course with different instructors. Ask about different instructors' lecture styles, test content and difficulty, course work load, and areas of emphasis in psychology.

Participating in Research Studies

In many introductory psychology courses, students are urged to participate in one or more psychology experiments. At most larger universities, psychology instructors not only teach, but they also conduct research. This research provides much of the information in your textbook. In order to do the research, the researchers need people to serve as subjects or participants. This is where you come in. Don't worry: they will not do anything unpleasant to you, like hooking electrodes to your brain or testing unknown drugs on you. You will always be informed ahead of time about anything stressful that might occur during the experiment, and you are free to leave at any time without losing your credit for participating.

Why Should You Participate in Psychology Experiments? The option to participate may be presented to you for extra credit toward your grade. In addition to benefits to your grade, though, you will gain some insight into how psychologists think and how psychology experiments are conducted. This insight may help you understand how much of the information in your textbook was discovered in the first place. Also, you will be making a contribution to research. If you absolutely do not wish to participate in experiments, however, the

TABLE 1.2 WHAT TO LOOK FOR IN THE SYLLABUS

1. Who is your instructor? Where is his or her office? What are the office hours? The phone number?
2. What textbook(s) is/are required?
3. What are the course objectives? How does the instructor describe the course?
4. What are the course requirements? How is your grade determined? What kind of tests will you have? How many? When? What percentage of your total grade is each test worth? Can you make up tests/quizzes? Is extra credit a possibility?
5. What is the attendance policy?
6. What are the reading assignments? How much reading will you have to do on a weekly basis? Will you have to read every chapter in the textbook?

Important. If any of this information is not included in the syllabus, you have the right to ask about it. Knowing this information will help you plan for studying and test preparation during the semester.

instructor will probably provide you with an alternative way to achieve extra credit, such as a library project.

GETTING MOTIVATED: GOOD REASONS TO STUDY PSYCHOLOGY

▪

Personal Learning Questions

Are you easily motivated? Are you motivated to do well in psychology? Why or why not?

▪

Nothing is more important to your success in this or any other class than motivation. If you are going to excel in this class (and in college in general), you must have, or find, motivation.

It's Your Future

To begin with, let's examine the most practical motivator for putting your time and sweat into introductory psychology: your future. Nothing is inherently evil about being an unmotivated person. However, if you are unmotivated to learn, you are likely to end up working for someone else at a job that you may not feel is very enjoyable or interesting.

The point that we are trying to make is that you should be motivated to do well in your classes ... not because we say so, and not because your parents or instructors say so, but because it is your life that will be affected by your grade point average and whether you graduate. The simple truth is, the more education you have and the higher your grades, the more freedom you will have in choosing what it is you are going to do for a living. If your motivation starts to waver, just picture yourself at age 50 trapped in a job that you hate and find boring and unchallenging. The four or so years that you will spend in college are going to have a dramatic impact on the forty or so working years that follow.

Intrinsic and Extrinsic Motivation

Your psychology textbook will discuss two different types of motivation: intrinsic and extrinsic. Being **intrinsically motivated** means you want to do something purely because of the enjoyment you get from doing it. If you read a book because it is a good book and you are enjoying it, you are intrinsically motivated to read that book.

You are **extrinsically motivated** if you do something because of some external reward you receive for doing it. If you read a book because it is required for an English course and you hope that you will eventually be rewarded for reading the book by getting an A, you are extrinsically motivated to read the book. If you are motivated to get an A in psychology because you want a high grade-point average so that you can get a good, enjoyable job when you graduate, you are extrinsically motivated to get an A in psychology.

Certainly, nothing is wrong with working hard solely for the prospect of a brighter future. And although in most cases a combination of intrinsic and extrinsic motivational factors influences behavior, the more effective kind of motivation is intrinsic motivation. If you can get interested in a class to the point that you might go to it even if you were not getting credit for it, you will find the class will be much easier. When you are really interested in the subject matter, it is easier to pay attention and to remember details. It is also a lot more pleasant.

Intrinsic Motivation If you are not initially interested in psychology, faking an interest may lead to developing a real interest.

When one of the authors was a freshman in college, a friend of his told him that the way to keep a boring class from becoming torturous is to pretend that everything being said in the class is the most interesting thing you have ever heard. We know what you are thinking: "Sure, that's fine for a day, but you can only fake interest for so long." Well, here's another story!

A friend of ours hated the fact that her husband was a hockey fanatic. He went to hockey games all the time, leaving her home alone. One day she confided that she was going to start faking an interest in hockey so she could spend more time with her husband. A few months later, she called us on the phone, crying because her hockey team had just lost the Stanley Cup championship. Where was her husband? He was at work. She was watching the game alone!

Our interests, what music we like and what hobbies we like, are typically not there when we are born. We choose them. Fortunately, psychology is extremely interesting. Many students find it interesting with little or no effort. Psychology appeals to most of us because we have a healthy interest in our own thoughts, behaviors, beliefs, and fears. Beyond just being interesting to us, psychology is useful: It provides information that can be used in our day-to-day lives.

For example, you will learn about **interpersonal attraction.** If you are at a college campus that is away from your family and long-time friends, you may be trying to make new social contacts. If this is the case, it can be helpful to understand what influences the people we like and the ones we do not. This is what interpersonal attraction is all about.

Psychology in Real Life: How to Be Liked

What influences **liking?** Liking is a well-researched topic in psychology. As we mentioned earlier regarding dating relationships, we like people who are similar to us in interests, background, and so on. We also like people who are attractive.[3] People who are models are at an unfair advantage when it comes to making friends, but part of being attractive is under our control. Part of liking attractive people is liking people who take pride in their appearance. We like people who are well dressed and well-groomed more than people who take little care in their appearance. This finding suggests that it helps to look our best when trying to make new friends.

Believe it or not, we do not particularly like people who do us favors.[4] This is especially true if we feel that the favor is a "bribe" for our friendship, or if we feel that we are being obligated to return the favor. We do, however, like people who ask us for a favor (assuming that the favor is not a big inconvenience). Most of us feel good about helping others, even in small ways, and we appreciate it when someone singles us out as being competent to help. Based on this finding, a good way to initiate a friendship with someone is to ask him or her to help you with something you do not understand in class. Finally, we like people who like us.[5] It is more likely that someone will express an interest in being friends with us if we make our liking for that person known to him or her.

---

[3] E. Hatfield and S. Sprecher, *Mirror, Mirror... The Importance of Looks in Everyday Life* (Albany, NY: State University of New York Press, 1986.)

[4] A. Nadler and J. D. Fisher, The Role of Threat to Self-esteem and Perceived Control in Recipient Reactions to Help: Theory Development and Empirical Validation, in *Advances in Experimental Social Psychology,* ed. L. Berkowitz (New York: Academic Press, 1986), Vol. 19, pp. 81–122.

[5] V. S. Folkes and D. D. Sears, Does Everybody Like a Liker? *Journal of Experimental Social Psychology, 13,* 1977, 505–519.

Psychology in Real Life: Dealing with Depression

Here's another example of information you will learn in your psychology class you can use in your life. While studying psychological disorders, you will learn about the causes, symptoms, and treatment of **depression.** This information is likely to be useful because depression is the most common psychological disorder. It is extremely likely that you or someone close to you will experience severe depression at some time in your life. If depression does enter your life in some way, a psychology course will arm you with useful information about the disorder. You will learn to recognize the symptoms: trouble sleeping (or sleeping too much), eating too little or too much, having little energy, having repetitive and negative thoughts, having no interest in anything, and, sometimes, having thoughts of suicide.

You will also learn that depression is often caused by some major loss in a person's life, such as a divorce, the death of a family member or friend, or flunking out of school. Finally, you will learn how depression is treated. Anti-depressant medication and therapy can help. But depression always goes away eventually with or without psychological help, though it is likely to recur from time to time in the lives of people who suffer from it. Most importantly, you will learn that suicide attempts are not uncommon among people suffering from depression, and this knowledge might save someone's life.

We do not want to give away all of the useful information that your instructor and psychology text have to offer. We just want to make you aware that your effort in this class will return not only a good grade but some worthwhile information as well. Besides the two examples we have mentioned, the application of psychological principles can help you resist or make sales pitches, become informed about better parenting, be healthier, improve your problem-solving abilities, understand others' behaviors, be happier, and many other things.

Extrinsic Motivation What can you do if you absolutely cannot develop an interest in psychology, or some other class? You go to the next best thing: extrinsic motivation. Extrinsic motivation works on the time-tested principle that when we are rewarded for doing something, we will keep doing it, and when we are punished for doing something, we will stop doing it.

If you find a class or a topic boring, set up a way to reward yourself for studying it. If you love reading Stephen King novels, for example, then when you get his latest book, make a deal with yourself that you can read a chapter only after you study for the boring class for an hour. Extrinsic motivation works well to keep you going through work that you do not like doing.

By the way, this information on extrinsic motivation has just introduced you to the concept of **operant conditioning.** Operant conditioning is based on the simple principle that people (and animals) will learn to repeat behaviors that bring good results (like rewards) and will learn to avoid behaviors that bring bad results (like punishments). You will be seeing a lot of material on operant conditioning both in this book and in your course, so try to stay familiar with the concept.

Motivation and Perseverance

One final thought on motivation. One of the most common ways that motivation gets crushed is through failure. We get psyched up and motivated to do well in something, but then we fail on our first couple of attempts, which gets us discouraged. If you think you have had your share of failure, take a look at this man's life:

Portrait of a Failure

Failed twice in business.
Defeated for election to the legislature.
Fiancee dies.
Defeated for Speaker.
Defeated for Elector.
Marries, three of four sons die by age 18.
Defeated for Congress twice.
Defeated for Senate twice.
Defeated for Vice President.

It seems like everyone in this man's life either died or voted against him. You would think that someone who experienced so much failure and bad luck would get the message and hang it up. But this particular person did not. In fact, this person ended up being elected President. This loser was Abraham Lincoln.

The point that we are trying to make is that the person who is most likely to be successful is not the person with the most talent but the person who can take the most failure and still get up, brush off the dust, and continue on. Failure can be useful because it gives you feedback about what you should do differently next time. If you take failure too personally, however, it steals your motivation and can wither away your spirit. Perseverance is a powerful ally. If you can teach yourself to let moments of failure glance off you, then you can never really be finally defeated. This lesson is not just true in school and in work—it is true in everything.

> *"Satisfaction lies in the effort, not the attainment. Full effort is full victory."*
>
> —Gandhi

APPLICATION EXERCISES

1. Why are you taking Introduction to Psychology? Brainstorm for a few minutes and list the reasons why you are taking this course.

   ____

   ____

   ____

   ____

   Now, mark IM (intrinsic motivation) or EM (extrinsic motivation), whichever is appropriate, over each reason you listed. Are you more intrinsically or extrinsically motivated to take psychology?

   ____

   Knowing the kind of motivation you feel at this point in the semester may help you keep focused, develop an interest, or set up a reward system for yourself.

2. Identify two rewards that would each motivate you to do one hour of classwork that you don't want to do.

   ____

   ____

3. How are you going to reward yourself for completing this chapter?

____

____

____

____

TERMS TO KNOW

classical conditioning
depression
extrinsic motivation
interpersonal attraction
intrinsic motivation
liking
motivation
operant conditioning
Pavlov

CHAPTER 2

PSYCHOLOGY: The Big Picture

GETTING FOCUSED

- *What is the "big picture" of psychology?*
- *What are the seven areas of psychology?*
- *How does your instructor think about psychology?*

▪

PERSONAL LEARNING QUESTIONS

What do you already know about psychology? What do psychologists study? How does knowledge of psychology affect your life? What do you already know about the psychology course you are taking this semester/quarter?

▪

Before we discuss how to read, study, and prepare for tests in psychology, you should first have a working knowledge of psychology itself. In this chapter, we will introduce you to the main topic areas in psychology. We will also explain some of the key concepts in each area. This overview should give you a head start in your class because you will be hearing and reading about these concepts often.

UNDERSTANDING THE BIG PICTURE: DEVELOPING A SCHEMA FOR PSYCHOLOGY

Before you dive in and start learning the specifics of psychology, it is important to get yourself familiar with the subject in a more general sense. Understanding the "big picture" can be a big help before you start learning the details, because it's much easier to learn facts if you can fit them into a larger context or framework. Getting the big picture is one of the keys to understanding and remembering. Remember facts within the overall picture, not as isolated tidbits of information. In the language of psychology, this overall context or "big picture" is called a **schema.**

The big picture in psychology is made up of several general areas. Some of these areas are very different from others. In fact, a psychologist who specializes in one area may not even understand what a psychologist in another area is talking about. Therefore, learning psychology is not like learning history, where each chapter continues the story from the previous chapter. Because psychology textbooks are organized by topic, rather than chronologically, the order of most of the chapters could be scrambled, and the book would still be understandable.

Psychology is made up of about seven general areas. We say "about" seven because some texts will name a few more or a few less, depending on how each author conceptualizes psychology. For our purposes here, let's stay with seven. The seven areas are:

1. Biological
2. General experimental
3. Cognitive
4. Developmental
5. Personality
6. Social
7. Clinical

Most of the chapters in your book will be included in one of these general areas. To get you oriented, in this chapter we are going to look at each of these areas and also at which chapters of your text come from which area.

Hint: Important Psychology Concepts to Know

In Appendix 1 at the end of the book, we provide explanations of some of the psychological concepts that are absolutely essential to each general area. You may want to skim this material now, but it will make more sense to you when you are reading your psychology textbook. For example, when you are reading about general experimental psychology in your textbook, refer to the "Important Concepts of General Experimental Psychology" section in Appendix 1 for a clear picture of the most important concepts, along with a few examples. We realize that many students ignore information appearing after the main body of a book, but please take advantage of the many hints and examples that we have included to help demystify important concepts in psychology. Take the time to look through Appendix 1 now so that you are aware of the kind of help available to you in this book.

The general areas here and the concepts in Appendix 1 should provide you with a good framework, or schema, for what psychology is all about. As you read, also take a quick look at the figure on page 26, which is an illustration of the seven areas. Using graphics such as this one is a way to organize information to learn it more easily. We will talk more about how you can create your own, more detailed graphics in Chapters 5 (The Language of Psychology) and 7 (Studying Psychology).

THE SEVEN AREAS OF PSYCHOLOGY

Below you will find descriptions of the seven areas of psychology and the kinds of chapter titles you will find in your textbook in each area. We also make some general recommendations about how you might consider studying the material in each area.

Biological Psychology

Description The area of **biological psychology** looks at the brain, the nervous system, cells, and hormones to explain why we do what we do. In other words, it tries to explain our behavior by looking at our bodies. For example, in order to figure out why people sometimes experience depression, a biological psychologist might try to find out if there is something wrong with the person's brain or whether a chemical imbalance causes depression.

Chapters The chapter in your textbook that deals with biological psychology is probably titled something like "Brain and Behavior" or

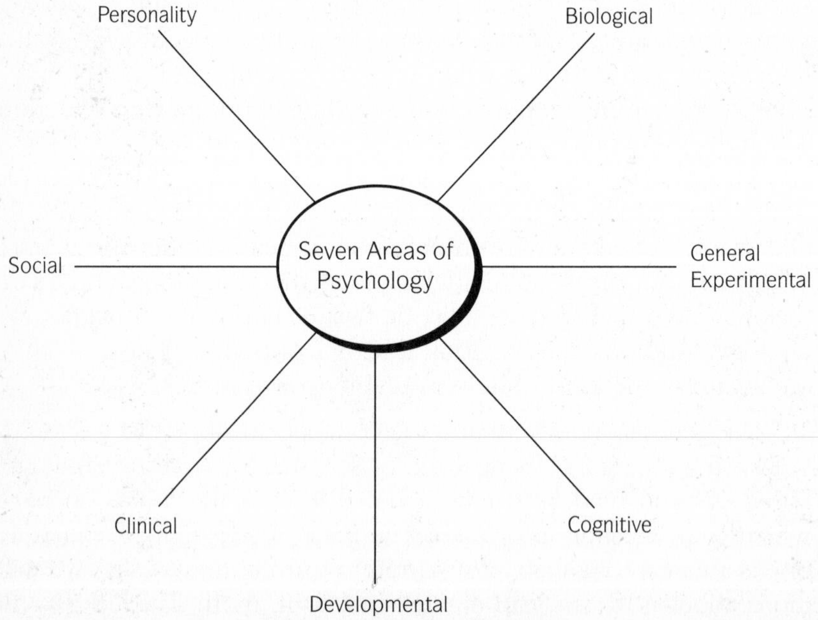

The Seven Areas of Psychology

"Biological Bases of Behavior." It covers exactly what we have described above. You may also come across biological psychology in chapters on "Sensation and Perception" and "Motivation and Emotion," but these chapters are more directly related to the next area.

Which chapters in your textbook appear to deal with biological psychology?

____

____

____

____

Studying Considerations Because most of the information in this area has a strong emphasis on biological science, you can expect to encounter many new and unfamiliar technical terms. Therefore, memory tricks such as imagery and acronyms, structural analysis, and a vocabulary learning strategy such as vocabulary cards will be useful for learning the new terminology. In addition, you will probably have to interpret several illustrations that depict phenomena in the nervous system, brain, and cells, for example. You may want to recreate some of the drawings in order to understand where specific structures are located. Memory strategies are key to understanding and remembering information in biological psychology.

General Experimental Psychology

Description The area of **general experimental psychology** is the study of basic behaviors that are shared by all animals (including humans), such as sex, hunger, basic learning, sensation and perception, and aggression. General experimental psychologists often work with animals such as monkeys and white rats.

Chapters Usually, your textbook will contain a few chapters that deal with general experimental psychology. "Sensation and Perception" looks at our five senses and how we use them to understand what is going on in the world. Such a chapter covers information like how the eyes work and why optical illusions trick us. "Learning" examines different types of basic learning, especially two types called **operant conditioning** and **classical conditioning.** A chapter with this title is not about the kind of learning that you do in college. Instead, it is about very basic learning, such as how we learn not to stick our fingers in electrical sockets and how rats learn to run mazes. "Motivation and Emotion" covers just what you would imagine: What is it that motivates us to do what we do? You will look at basic motives like hunger and sex and more sophisticated ones such as the desires for love and achievement. You will also look at theories of why we have emotions and what emotions do to us. Usually, not much time is spent looking at specific emotions, such as jealousy, fear, or anger. The focus will be on emotions in general.

Which chapters in your textbook appear to deal with general experimental psychology?

____

____

____

Studying Considerations A "Sensation and Perception" chapter usually has a strong biological emphasis, so the considerations suggested previously in biological psychology are also relevant here. A "Learning" chapter contains concepts, such as classical and operant conditioning, that can be confusing to introductory psychology students; thus, it is helpful to use vocabulary strategies and to create several different examples to illustrate and make sure you understand the concepts. An "Emotions" chapter usually presents theories about emotions, and it is helpful to use mapping and other graphic displays in order to understand and learn theories. "Motivation" is often a combination of material, some of which lends itself well to mapping (e.g., styles of love and achievement), and some of which have a strong biological emphasis (e.g., hunger and thirst), thus lending itself well to vocabulary learning strategies and recreation of drawings.

Cognitive Psychology

Description The area of **cognitive psychology** studies thinking, that is, how we think about things, how we solve problems. Cognitive psychologists often compare the mind to a computer and talk about thinking as **information processing.** Information processing refers to the whole process by which we take information from the outside world, interpret it, use it, and store it.

Chapters Several chapters may deal with cognitive psychology. "Thinking" examines how we think, how we solve problems, and how we make decisions. One of the points often mentioned is that we aren't as good at thinking as we think we are! People make many mistakes when they are trying to think something through or solve some problem. "Memory" usually makes two main points: how memory works and how you can make your memory better. "Language" is another aspect of cognitive psychology, because, in a sense, language is thinking out loud. How we use language and how language is structured are the major issues covered. "Intelligence" asks questions such as these: "Is intelligence one thing, or can people be intelligent in some ways and unintelligent in others?" "Are IQ tests really a good measure of intelligence?" "Do we inherit our smarts from our parents, or does our upbringing determine how intelligent we become?"

Which chapters in your textbook appear to deal with cognitive psychology?

___

___

___

Studying Considerations Mapping and other graphic displays are useful strategies for studying material in nearly all the cognitive psychology chapters because there are several complex concepts that map well (e.g., characteristics of short- and long-term memory, theories of forgetting, characteristics of personality related to creativity and intelligence, and theories about the influence of language on thought).

Developmental Psychology

Description The area of **developmental psychology** looks at how we change as we get older. Because most of the changes we go through take place when we are children, much of development is about children.

Chapters Development looks at two areas: "Child Development" and "Adult Development." The former examines children's physical, cognitive, and emotional growth, such as how infants get better muscle coordination as they get older and how children get better at solving problems as they get older. "Adult Development" examines life changes like marriage, having children, and aging.

Which chapters in your textbook appear to deal with developmental psychology?

Studying Considerations Developmental psychology contains information that requires the use of several strategies. Timelines work well when dealing with chronology and sequence, as development does. Also, there are usually many technical terms that you can learn using vocabulary cards and imagery. Theories of physical, cognitive, social, and moral development throughout the lifespan lend themselves well to mapping.

Personality Psychology

Description The area of **personality psychology** looks at how and why people differ from each other. Why are some people shy and some outgoing? Why are some people leaders and some followers?

Chapters Usually, there is just one chapter on personality, covering a number of different personality theories. Freud's theory of personality is one of the main theories. The key to this chapter is understanding how all the theories differ from each other. The chapter on personality may be thought of as a debate among psychologists who have different ideas about how we get to be who we are.

Which chapters in your textbook appear to deal with personality psychology?

Studying Considerations Personality psychology is similar to developmental psychology in that the variety of information presented requires you to utilize a variety of strategies for effective learning. Because of the many theories and terms in personality psychology, mapping, comparing and contrasting, and vocabulary strategies are important. Timelines may be of use if it is necessary for you to be familiar with the historical development of the theories.

Social Psychology

Description The area of **social psychology** studies interactions among people. If a topic involves two or more people doing something together, it is probably social psychology. Love, violence, conformity, and competition are all topics in social psychology.

Chapters A chapter on "Social Cognition" is concerned with how we think about other people and about the social world in general. (Remember that cognition deals with thoughts, or thinking about things.) How we stereotype other people also would be discussed because it involves thinking about groups of people. Our attitudes about others is another important topic in this area. "Social Interaction" involves actual interaction between people and examines issues of conformity, aggression, helping, and love.

Which chapters in your textbook appear to deal with social psychology?

____

____

____

Studying Considerations You will probably need to learn key studies in social psychology that demonstrate how humans react to different social situations. Thus, a mapping strategy that would focus on each of several issues, such as prejudice, conformity, attributions, attitudes, and roles, and their key studies, would probably be most useful.

Clinical Psychology

Description The area of **clinical psychology** is the area with which you are probably most familiar. Clinical psychologists provide therapy for patients. They treat people who are having psychological problems, such as depression or anxiety attacks.

Chapters Nearly all psychology textbooks contain a chapter on "Abnormal Psychology" (also sometimes called "Psychological disorders" or "Psychopathology") which looks at different types of mental illness, including the causes and the symptoms. Another chapter, "Therapy," may deal with treating mental illness. Because there are many different types of therapy, considerable time is spent evaluating how effective they are and comparing them to each other. You will meet some old friends from the personality chapter, like Freud and the behaviorists.

Which of the chapters in your textbook appear to deal with clinical psychology?

____

____

____

Studying Considerations Once again, mapping will help you understand more thoroughly the differences between types of therapies. A vocabulary strategy and imagery will aid you in learning the names and characteristics of the various mental illnesses.

We hope that you now have a better handle on what you'll be learning over the next few months. Try to keep this "big picture" in mind as you start getting into the details, so that you have a way to organize them. Now that you have a working knowledge of how psychology is organized and what some of the main concepts are, let's look at how your instructor views psychology.

HOW YOUR INSTRUCTOR MAY THINK ABOUT PSYCHOLOGY

By considering how your psychology instructor thinks about this material, you will better be able to follow the lectures and to predict what the instructor may think is important enough to put on a test.

Psychologists Are Scientists

First and foremost, psychologists are scientists. They tend to believe that psychology is related more closely to biology, physics, and chemistry than to art, English, and history. What this means to you is that your psychology instructor is likely to emphasize scientific facts when testing you. If information is presented as not supported by scientific research or theory, it is less likely that your instructor expects you to know it. This hint is just a guideline and will not always be true, but it may help you to decide which information is most important to learn.

For example, during a lecture on sleep and dreams, your instructor may tell you that the dream stage of sleep is called **REM sleep.** REM is short for **r**apid **e**ye **m**ovement. Your instructor will likely tell you that REM sleep is accompanied by the following symptoms: rapid eye movement under the eyelids, more brain activity and a higher heart rate than during other stages of sleep, and muscle paralysis. These are scientific facts. To make the material relevant and interesting, your instructor may include some interesting anecdotes or examples along with these facts about dream sleep. Maybe your instructor will tell you about a friend who suffered from nightmares, or that we really do not die if we dream that we die. The anecdotes and examples that an instructor adds to the bare facts are interesting and can help you remember the facts, but it is less likely that they will appear as test questions.

Psychologists Emphasize Experiments

For the most part, psychological facts are discovered by conducting psychological experiments. Because of the importance that your instructor places on psychology being scientific, you may find that she or he places a lot of emphasis on the actual experiments that were conducted to learn those psychological facts.

We know, for example, that most people will obey authority, even if it means doing something that they think is wrong. This is a scientific fact. The suggestion that most people will blindly obey authority was demonstrated in an experiment conducted by Stanley Milgram, a social psychologist.[1] He led people to believe that they were giving electrical shocks to a man in another room as part of an experiment on memory. Each time the man in the next room answered a question incorrectly, the subject was instructed by a psychologist in a white lab coat to give the man a shock by pressing a lever. The shocks became stronger with each wrong answer, and soon the man in the next room was screaming in pain. In reality, the man in the other room was working for Milgram and was only pretending to receive the shocks. Whenever the shock-delivering subject hesitated or questioned the safety of shocking the man in the other room (who mentioned at the outset that he had a heart condition), the experimenter would calmly but firmly tell him or her to continue with the experiment.

---

[1] S. Milgram, "Behavior Study of Obedience," *Journal of Abnormal and Social Psychology,* 67, (1963), 371–378.

By the end of the experiment, the shocks that the subjects thought they were delivering were of extremely high voltage, and the man in the next room was no longer making any sound at all. Yet 65% of the people that Milgram tested continued the shocks under the pressure of the psychologist, even though they thought that they were hurting, or even killing, the man in the next room. The subjects obeyed the person in authority, even if they thought what they were doing was wrong.

Incidentally, it was because of studies like these that colleges and universities began to place limits on experiments and student participation. Therefore, you should not fear participating in experiments for your psychology class.

In general, most psychologists are taught that experiments are the foundation of psychology, and it will probably benefit you to keep this idea in mind.

Psychologists Often Specialize

To get a bearing on how your instructor thinks about psychology, you should also find out your instructor's primary area of interest. You can find out your instructor's specialty by asking. As we mentioned earlier, psychology is a broad field, and many psychologists are only trained extensively in one general area. Specializing does not mean that they are ignorant of the other areas. It means that they are more knowledgeable (and usually more interested) in their particular area of expertise.

For example, if your instructor is a clinical psychologist, he or she may emphasize psychological disorders and therapy more than other areas. If your instructor is a general experimentalist, he or she is likely to emphasize sensation and perception, learning, and animal behavior.

That is the "big picture" of psychology. Remember that our goal in providing you with this overview is not to tell you every bit of information you will need to know to do well on tests, but to provide you with a foundation and a schema that you can build upon. The next step is to give you the tools to more efficiently and effectively learn the information that you will encounter in your psychology text and class.

APPLICATION EXERCISES

1. Did your general examination of the titles of the chapters in your psychology book remind you of what else you already know about psychology? Do you know more or less than you originally thought?

   ____

   ____

2. What areas interest you the most?

   ____

   ____

   Remember those areas, and use this interest as motivation to study.

TERMS TO KNOW

biological psychology
classical conditioning
clinical psychology
cognitive psychology
developmental psychology
general experimental psychology
information processing
operant conditioning
personality psychology
REM sleep
schema
social psychology

CHAPTER 3

READING PSYCHOLOGY

GETTING FOCUSED

- *How can you preview your psychology textbook?*
- *What is brainstorming?*
- *How do you examine the structure and contents of an assignment?*
- *How can you decide how much to read each time you read?*
- *What is active reading?*
- *How can you mark your text using annotation?*
- *How do you analyze your annotations?*

▪

Personal Learning Questions

How do you usually read textbook assignments? What difficulties do you experience when:

- **learning new vocabulary?**
- **figuring out what is important to know?**
- **understanding how the concepts relate to each other?**

▪

It's time to open your psychology book and examine in more detail what lies ahead of you in psychology this semester. In this chapter, we will look at what you can do to prepare to read your psychology text, distinguish between what is and is not important in the text while you read, monitor your understanding of what you read, and store the important information to study at a later time (see Chapters 7 and 8).

PREVIEWING YOUR TEXTBOOK

Before you start to read your first assignment in psychology (or in any course, for that matter), you can get a lot of information about the course by examining the whole book. Follow the activities listed on the chart that will help you thoroughly preview your textbook.

PREVIEWING YOUR TEXTBOOK
1. Page through the entire text. Get an overall picture. 2. Examine the title page and copyright. 3. Examine the tables of contents. 4. Figure out the organization and main topics of the textbook.

1. Turn the pages of your psychology text to get a feel for its appearance and format. Are there many pictures, or are most pages filled with text?

   ____

   ____

2. Do any topics grab your interest? If so, which one(s)?

____

____

____

3. How do you feel when you look through the book—interested, bored, curious, skeptical, or full of dread?

____

____

(Find something that looks interesting and skim it, just to motivate yourself for the course if you are not already motivated.)

4. How many pages does the book have?

____

Most introductory psychology books are approximately 700 pages long, depending on the size of the print and pages. (The glossary and appendices usually add another one or two hundred pages to the text.).

5. Who is/are the author(s)?

____

6. What university is each author from?

____

(You never know: it could be your instructor and your university.)

7. Turn to the table of contents. Actually, you may find two tables of contents. If your text has two, the first one is usually a broad overview that just lists the titles of each major part of the book and the titles of chapters. The second table of contents goes into much more depth about what is in each chapter.

As we discussed in Chapter 2, nearly every psychology book covers approximately seven areas: biological, general experimental, cognitive, developmental, personality, social, and clinical. The units and/or chapters in your text might not be called exactly by those names, but if you look at the listing of the contents of each chapter, you will probably find most of these categories.

Take a couple of minutes with the table of contents to examine what you will be reading. While you are doing this, you may also want to take out your course syllabus. Has your instructor assigned every chapter in the book or just a few? Put a check mark or star in the table of contents by the chapters that you are assigned to read, and take an extra look at what you will be reading about in those chapters.

▪

PERSONAL LEARNING QUESTIONS

What is your overall impression of your psychology text?
How easy or difficult do you think it will be to read it?

▪

PREREADING CONSIDERATIONS

What you do before you read an assigned chapter is almost as important as what you do while you read. Before you read, you need to think about what you already know about the topic at hand, examine the structure and content of the assignment, and decide how much and when you will read. Take the time before you read to plan your strategy: Doing so will make learning and studying easier in the long run.

Know What You Know: Brainstorm

If you think about what you already know about a topic before you read, it is much easier to learn and organize new information about that topic. Remember when we talked about a schema in Chapter 2? A schema is a framework you have for a particular topic. You have a schema for birthdays, for pencils, for dogs, for restaurants, and for Wankel rotary engines. You have a schema for everything you have ever experienced or have read or heard about, and you are constantly revising and changing your schemata (plural) as you gain new information.

For example, most of us have a schema for checking out at a grocery store. You (or a store worker) may empty the contents of your cart onto the conveyor belt, and the cashier totals the cost of your purchases and puts the items in bags. There may be an electronic eye that scans the code on the item to register a description and price, or at an older store the cashier may key in the price by hand. In the past, groceries were placed only in paper bags. Now, we have a choice of paper or plastic. We know that we usually wait for the cash register slip before we leave. We may take the groceries out in the cart to the car, or a grocery store worker may do it for us.

When one of the authors first moved to Louisiana, she went to a large grocery store to stock the kitchen of her new apartment. As she was standing in the check-out line, she kept hearing a droning voice saying something very repetitive. When she got up to the cashier, she realized that the voice was coming from the cash register: "$1.49," "$1.88," "$7.89," and so on, saying the price of each item as the electric eye scanned the code. She revised her grocery store schema to include talking cash registers. The next time she heard the voice, she was not surprised, and she did not have to relearn the fact.

This is a simple example, with very little of importance riding on whether or not we remember that talking cash registers exist in this world. However, the same principles apply when you are reading and studying. New information "hooks onto" the framework or schema that you already have for a topic, based on previously acquired information, making it much easier to learn and remember. (Keep in mind, however, that your schema may contain inaccurate information, so you will want to be very careful when reading and studying to identify and correct any misconceptions you may have learned.) The previous overview of psychology for example, should give you an overall schema of psychology that will make new information easier to learn and remember.

When you start to read a chapter in any textbook, get your existing schema for the topic up and running and ready for expansion by **brainstorming** about everything you know about the topic. If you simply plunge into the chapter on emotions, for example, without thinking about what you already know about them, you make your job of learning and remembering much more difficult. Because you usually have a schema for nearly every topic in psychology, activate one or more as you read a chapter.

Imagine that your instructor has assigned the chapter "Emotion." Before you start reading, brainstorm: What do you already know about emotions? For example:

1. Are you an emotional person or do you know someone who is? What is a person like who is "emotional"?

2. How do you feel when you are angry or upset? What physical feelings do you have?

3. How do you feel when you are happy?

4. Think about how difficult it can be to act rationally when you are experiencing overwhelming emotions such as grief or fear. Does anything else come to mind when you think about emotions?

(Keep brainstorming if you're on a roll. If not, you are now ready to look at the chapter on emotions.)

Examine the Structure and Contents of the Assignment

Contrary to what most people do when they begin reading a textbook, you do not start reading the first page and go straight through until you are done. Turn to the chapter on emotions in your own textbook, and we will comment on a similar chapter in a textbook that we are using. We will walk you through the chapter and show you what to expect, knowing that you will probably be tested on this material at some point.

1. First, how long is the chapter?

   ____

   (Ours is about 30 pages long.)

   Does the chapter seem very long to you? If so, take heart. We will suggest a simple way to make your way through the material more effectively and less painfully.

2. What do the pages look like? That is, are there any pictures, boxes, charts, or graphs to break up the text? Briefly describe what you see.

   ____

   ____

   ____

   (Ours only has a picture on every other page or so.)

3. How is the chapter divided? That is, how many sections does it have?

   ____

   Most chapters are divided logically into sections using headings and subheadings. To get an overview of the chapter in one glance, you can look at the headings and subheadings as they are listed in the table of contents at the beginning of the book or, if provided, in a listing on the first page of the chapter.

4. Approximately how many pages are in each section?

   ____

   (Ours has about seven.)

5. What are these sections about? Page through each section. What pops out at you?

   ____

   ____

   ____

The purpose of this activity is to see what you will be learning and to see if you already know something about the topic that you did not recall when you were brainstorming earlier. Listen to what we do as we look at the sections in our chapter on emotions.[1] Imagine that you are eavesdropping on us as we think aloud.

Example: Brainstorming and Developing Interest in Emotions

"For the most part, each section in this chapter deals with the 'Elements of Emotion'—body, mind, and culture—and then a last section discusses all three as they relate to gender. That's interesting. We suppose they will discuss overgeneralizations about how women are more emotional than men. Because we're interested in gender issues, we are going to try to get psyched to read this chapter by skimming that section…hmmm, it does not look sexist at all. It talks about both genders, how and when they express emotions, and how different jobs require different emotions. Our interest is piqued enough to want to read this chapter.

"But next we need to take a closer look at the subheadings and boldfaced words in the text and see if we know more about emotions than we initially thought. The first major section is about emotions and the body—we know that they are interrelated somehow. The text presents a few different theories about this relationship, so it appears that there is not a clear-cut answer to the question 'Which came first, the emotion or the physical feeling?' Then, the section looks at how emotions are expressed on people's faces and how that is an important part of communication. Well, that's true; sometimes all you have to do is look at people to know how they feel, and sometimes what they look like and what they are saying are two separate things. Now, the text discusses what the body experiences in an intense emotion—we can relate to that because we feel our emotions strongly when we are angry or scared. Now, the book goes into emotions, the brain, and how lie detector tests measure bodily changes when a person lies.

"In the second major section, the text deals with the emotions and the mind, how thoughts affect emotions and how you can get yourself all worked up and upset about something just by thinking about it. Next, the text talks about how we can feel two or more emotions at the same time, like hope and fear (example: what you might feel when you take a test), and how the same experience can prompt different people to feel different emotions or degrees of the same emotion.

---

[1]Excerpts from *Psychology,* 2nd ed., by Carole Wade and Carol Travis. Copyright © 1989 by Harper & Row, Publishers, Inc., Reprinted by permission of HarperCollins, Inc.

"The third section is about emotions and culture and how what makes us angry in our culture might not make people in another culture the least bit upset. We did not know that! It looks like there are positive and negative emotions (not a big surprise), and also primary and secondary emotions (something of a surprise). Wonder what they are? Now there is a discussion of which emotions are appropriate to express in our culture and which ones are not. Here is a mention of body language and how body language can show both emotion and status. Personally, we notice the relationship of body language, emotion, and status more between men and women than we do between cultures.

"We have already looked at the fourth section on the emotions and gender. Overall, there were approximately 15 boldfaced words, so the vocabulary load will not be too heavy. This chapter looks interesting, and we know more about emotions than we thought we did. Still, it looks like there are many studies that explore this topic quite deeply, and that information makes up the bulk of the information in this chapter."

What You Learn When You Preread a Chapter

You can learn a lot when you examine a chapter before you read it. First, you can see what you are getting into; that is, the length, difficulty, and structure of the material give you an idea of how much time and effort you will have to put into reading the material, and how you may best learn it. For example, the length and difficulty of the material will determine when and how much time you will need to allot for reading and studying. If there is a heavy vocabulary load, such as in a chapter on the brain, you will need to use different learning strategies than if the vocabulary load is light or if there are several theories to compare and contrast, such as in a chapter on personality.

Second, you may find that you already know something about the topic, and, as we have already discussed, it's easier to learn new information when you think about what you already know. Finally, you may find something in the chapter that you can personally relate to, which makes learning easier and more meaningful. For example, we found that our emotions chapter had a section on emotions and gender, an area of great personal interest to us—now, we have a personally motivating reason to read the chapter. You are more likely to read and pay attention to what you read when you find a reason to care about learning besides doing well on the test.

Whenever you begin a new chapter, page through it and discover what you're getting into, how much you already know, how you will have to study in the near future, and what will motivate you personally about the material.

Break Up the Amount You Read in One Sitting

You are almost ready to start reading. How much time you take to read the chapter depends on how much time you have left yourself to finish this chapter in time for class discussion or lecture and/or a test. In some classes, the instructor assigns a chapter or two per week and tests you on that material every week. In others, the instructor may say that the first test covers a certain number of chapters, and you have to figure out for yourself how you are going to read everything in time to study and be prepared for the test.

Regardless of your particular situation, regardless of how much or how little you have to read, never sit down and plow through the material from start to finish. You end up counting the pages and slogging along, wishing you were finished so you could relax, visit friends, or play basketball. Your attention will not be fully on the task at hand, and when you are not paying attention while you read, you might as well not read at all.

Instead of sitting down for a marathon session with the textbook, divide your reading into manageable chunks. For example, if we were assigned the emotions chapter previously discussed, in our first session we might just read the first major section of the chapter—seven pages sounds more "do-able" than the whole thirty. We can pay attention for the time it takes to read seven, but we will probably have difficulty keeping that kind of concentration for thirty pages. We will read and take notes on the seven pages, take a fifteen minute break, and read the next seven pages. That is probably all we will do on that chapter tonight. We will finish the last two sections tomorrow.

Now, it's your turn. Using either the emotions chapter for practice or the actual chapter you were assigned today, divide the chapter into manageable sections.

1. How many sections did you divide the chapter into?

   ____

2. On which days/nights will you read section 1? section 2? section 3? etc. For how long a period of time will you read? Record your plans on the chart below.

SECTION	PAGES	WHEN?	FOR HOW LONG?

All that previewing, looking at subheadings, thinking about what you already know about the topic, and dividing up the material into manageable chunks for reading does not take much time. Do not take more than five minutes or so (unless you are fascinated with the topic), or you are just putting off the inevitable.

If you have waited until the night before the test to read five chapters, however, this approach will not work, and cramming is not a time-tested solution, either. You should be in the final stages of rehearsing and reduction if the test is tomorrow. If you plan ahead and read ahead, most of the time you will be able to avoid the anxiety and disappointment of last-minute preparation.

PREVIEWING A READING ASSIGNMENT IN 5 MINUTES OR LESS

1. Know what you know about the topic before you start reading. Brainstorm. Call up your schema for the topic.
2. Examine the structure of the chapter. How long is the chapter? How is it divided? What are the headings and subheadings?
3. Examine the contents of the chapter. Are any of the topics familiar? Can you relate any of the information to your own life? What are the main areas that will be discussed?
4. What kind of material will you have to learn? Mainly new concepts/vocabulary? Theories? Facts?
5. Decide, using headings, how to divide up the chapter for manageable reading.

READING THE ASSIGNED MATERIAL: BE ACTIVE

When students start to read an assignment, they typically pick up their highlighter. Although most college students seem to believe that highlighting material while they read is effective, highlighting is actually one of the least effective strategies. Drop the yellow, pink, or green highlighter! Put the top on it, and place it back in your desk drawer. Using a highlighter is passive. It may not seem like it because you are holding a marker and running it over "important" sentences in your book... or paragraphs... or whole pages.

Say NO to highlighters!

That's the problem. A highlighter is not much better than just running your eyes over the words without thinking about what you are reading. You start out with the best of intentions, carefully highlighting definitions and theories. Soon, however, you get tired and become less discriminating. You begin highlighting more and more and more until whole pages are orange or yellow. Many students use the physical action of using the highlighter as a way to keep themselves from falling asleep and/or prove to themselves later that they "read" the chapter. With extensive highlighting, they are also usually unable to remember what they just read.

Why is it that they cannot remember what they just read? Because highlighting does not require you to pay attention or remember or learn. It also requires you to reread your highlights, and rereading is another passive strategy. In addition, you may have highlighted much more information than you needed. Because you have a lot to read in nearly every course you take, you do not have the time to go back and reread *and* study everything you highlighted.

The key to reliable reading, studying, and learning is to actively process the information. Active processing means that you do something with the material rather than just look at it. Reorganize the material, question it, relate it to some personal experiences of your own, make up a song about it—anything will work better than just repeating it or highlighting it. Some methods work better than others, however. Choosing the right strategies deserves careful consideration.

The annotation strategy almost always ends up being students' favorite method because it helps them remember more information and study more effectively, and it can be used in almost every course they take.

Becoming a Master Annotator

Annotation is an active reading strategy that requires you to make notes in the margins of your textbook as you read.[2] You only write and mark the important information or key ideas and their supporting details, thereby weeding out the rest, which, for the most part, is unnecessary for you to reread or learn.

As you take notes, put the information into your own words as much as possible. Copying the information exactly as the author worded it is passive. You will process the information more actively if you try to explain it to yourself and write it in your own words.

Along with selecting the important information, organize that information in a way that will make studying it at a later time much easier. Think back to schema theory (understanding a topic's framework): if you try to learn one isolated piece of information after another, you probably will not learn it very well. But if you organize the information and are aware how each piece fits into the "big picture," you learn and understand the material more thoroughly.

Learning to annotate a textbook well takes practice, patience, and attention. You may start off well, annotating very carefully and doing a good job. After a while, however, you get tired of thinking so hard, and you start getting sloppy. You leave out important information, or you start writing everything down even if it is not important. Being tired or bored leads you to be less selective. Remember how we divided up the emotions chapter into four major sections to read? Read and annotate just one section at a time, and you can handle it without getting bored or tired.

---

[2]Adapted from M. L. Simpson and S. L. Nist, "Textbook Annotation: An Effective and Efficient Study Strategy for College Students," *Journal of Reading,* 34, (1990), 122–129. Copyright by the International Reading Association.

HINTS FOR ANNOTATING YOUR TEXTBOOK

1. DO NOT USE A HIGHLIGHTER!
2. Read a few paragraphs or the whole section before annotating.
3. Pull out key ideas and significant supporting details.
4. Be brief.
5. Use your own words.
6. Use symbols and abbreviations.
7. Organize your annotations by labeling (and numbering, where appropriate).
8. Note examples.

Adapted from M. L. Simpson and S. L. Nist, "Textbook Annotation: An Effective and Efficient Study Strategy for College Students," *Journal of Reading,* 34 (1990), 122–129. Copyright by the International Reading Association.

"Okay," you may be saying to yourself at this point, "I'm willing to try annotation. But how do I know what to annotate?" Let us give you an example of one annotated page from the chapter on emotions in the psychology book that we have. Read the passage and the annotations that follow. Then take a closer look at what we chose to annotate (what we thought was important to learn) and how we annotated (abbreviations, phrases, and symbols).

ELEMENTS OF EMOTION: THE MIND[3]

A Bit of Background

1960s—Schachter & Singer *two-factor theory— emotion depends on 2 factors: 1) phys. arousal (what yr body feels) 2) cogn. interp. of arousal (how you label the feeling)	In the 1960s, Stanley Schachter and Jerome Singer proposed a **two-factor theory of emotion** (Schachter, 1971; Schachter & Singer, 1962). Bodily changes are necessary to experience an emotion, they said, but they are not enough. Your body may be churning away in high gear, but unless you can interpret, explain, and label those changes, you won't feel an "emotion." Schachter and Singer argued that true emotion depends on two factors: physiological arousal (the feeling of a feeling) and the cognitive

[3] Excerpt from *Psychology,* 2nd. ed. By Carol Wade and Carol Travis. Copyright 1989 by Harper & Row, Publishers, Inc. Reprinted by permission of HarperCollins, Inc.

3 predictions:
1) If aroused & not sure why, you will label the feeling [ex. pounding heart & nervous friends & exam → you must be nervous (but maybe not!)]

interpretation of that arousal (how you define what you are feeling). Three predictions follow from this theory:

1. *If you are physiologically aroused and don't know why, you will try to label your feeling, using interpretations of events around you.* If all your friends are nervous and worried about an upcoming exam, you may decide that the pounding of your heart is a sign that you are nervous, too. In fact, it may only be a result of your partying too much and not getting enough sleep.

2) If aroused & know why, no need to label [ex. ran 3 mi & pounding heart → not an emotion.]

2. *If (in the absence of an emotional event) you are physiologically aroused and you do know why—you have just been jogging for 3 miles and expect your pulse rate to be high-you will not feel a need to explain the changes in your body or to describe them as an emotion.*

3) If not aroused, interp will not produce emotion.

3. *If you are not physiologically aroused, your interpretations of events will not produce a true emotion.* You will react "emotionally" only when you are feeling some degree of arousal.

S&S—exp. to test theory.
– • diff. results than predicted
• hasn't been replicated.

To test these predictions, Schachter and Singer devised a clever experiment. It was so clever that psychologists love to tell about it, even though it didn't quite turn out as the experimenters hoped, and no one has been able to replicate the study (Marshall & Zimbardo, 1979; Maslach, 1979).

Exercise: Analyzing Annotation

Now, let's analyze the annotations we provided.

1. First, what is the passage about? Summarize the passage briefly before reading on.

    ____

    ____

    ____

    (We think that this passage is about Schachter and Singer's two-factor theory of emotion. A definition was given, followed by three predictions of the theory. An experiment to test the theory is mentioned.)

2. Now, what did we annotate? We pulled out: (1) the names of the experimenters, (2) the name of the theory, (3) a brief explanation of the theory, with specific factors numbered, (4) the three predictions, numbered, and (5) the experiment and two drawbacks to the experiment.

3. What didn't we annotate? We did not bother to annotate the second and third sentences because, after reading the whole paragraph, we realized that the definition of the theory was toward the end of the paragraph and that the second and third sentences just repeated the "real" definition. Most of the rest of the information was important enough to annotate, but we tried to reduce the amount of information by wording it more briefly.

4. Now, how did we annotate the important information? First, we wanted to be brief by using (1) abbreviations (like "phys" for *physiological,* "cogn" for *cognitive,* "interp" for *interpretation,* "S&S" for second mention of Schachter and Singer, etc.), (2) phrases rather than complete sentences, and (3) symbols, such as starring an important definition so that it will grab our attention later. Use a minus sign to indicate a problem, drawback, or disadvantage and a plus sign for advantages.

5. Next, we organized the information by (1) *labeling,* such as "emotion depends on two factors," and (2) *numbering* characteristics or factors. Labeling and numbering make it easier to organize your annotations for studying. If we had not organized them, when we went back to use or study our annotations, we would have had one isolated piece of information after another. When we organize, several pieces of information relate to each other, and we can study them as a *whole* rather than as one fact after another.

Exercise: Fill-in-the-Blanks in the Annotations

Now, it is your turn. On page 53, you will find another passage from the emotions chapter. We have given you the basic *organization* for the annotations, but left space for you to fill in the important information. Annotate the passage. Then, turn to page 54 to see how we completed the annotations, and compare yours with ours. Although everyone annotates differently, and one person may think something is important when another person does not, in general our key should be a pretty good guide. Please annotate page 53 now.

The varieties of emotion[4]

Varieties of Emotion

Process for naming emots:

1) Everyone distinguishes btwn ____ & ____ emotions

ex:

Some dist. only by ____

ex.

2) ____ & ____ emots.

a)

Identified by:

b)

Variation:

ex:

All cultures distinguish *positive* (pleasant) emotions from *negative* (unpleasant) ones (Storm & Storm, 1987; Watson, Clark & Tellegen, 1984). People everywhere regard love, joy, admiration and amusement as positive emotions, and they regard fear, hatred, sorrow, and shame as negative ones. A few cultures differentiate emotions only in terms of their negative or positive tone: some African tribes, for instance, have one word for "anger" and "sadness."

At the next level of emotion naming, most cultures recognize a number of **primary emotions,** which seem to be universal experiences. Psychologists distinguish these from **secondary emotions,** which include cultural variations (such as *schadenfreude* or *amaeru*), blends of feelings (the bittersweet emotion of feeling sad and happy at a friend's wedding, say), and degrees of intensity ("fear" can range from nervousness to terror) (J. Russell, 1983). Primary emotions have been identified in several ways: by universally recognized facial expressions; by the existence in most languages of words that label them; and by the predictable appearance of these emotions in child development. Thus the most common emotion words young children use are the basics: *happy, sad, mad,* and *scared.* As they get older, they learn varieties that are specific to their language, such as *ecstatic, depressed, hostile,* or *anxious* (Storm & Storm, 1987).

Depending on how psychologists go about measuring emotions, the list of the "primary" ones varies somewhat. Fear, anger, sadness, joy, surprise, and disgust turn up in most studies. But sometimes laypeople disagree with psychologists. Most Americans consider "love" to be an emotion, even though it doesn't have a typical facial expression (except perhaps the mooning gaze of new sweethearts). In contrast, they don't really think of surprise or disgust as true emotions, although both are registered on the face (Shaver et al., 1987; Storm & Storm, 1987).

[4]Excerpts from *Psychology,* 2nd ed., by Carole Wade and Carol Travis. Copyright © 1989 by Harper & Row, Publishers, Inc., Reprinted by permission of HarperCollins, Inc.

The varieties of emotion[4]

Varieties of Emotion
Process for naming emots:
1) Everyone distinguishes btwn positive & negative emotions
ex: love, joy, admir., amusement — fear, hatred, sorrow, shame
Some distinguish only by tone
ex: Afr. tribe—1 word for anger & sadness

2) primary and secondary emots.
   a) primary—universal
      Identified by:
      - facial expr.
      - words
      - appearance & dev. in humans
   b) secondary—cultural var
      - blends
      - ° of intensity

Variation:
Even primary emots. can vary w/in a culture
ex: love (no standard facial expres.)

All cultures distinguish *positive* (pleasant) emotions from *negative* (unpleasant) ones (Storm & Storm, 1987; Watson, Clark & Tellegen, 1984). People everywhere regard love, joy, admiration and amusement as positive emotions, and they regard fear, hatred, sorrow, and shame as negative ones. A few cultures differentiate emotions only in terms of their negative or positive tone: some African tribes, for instance, have one word for "anger" and "sadness."

At the next level of emotion naming, most cultures recognize a number of **primary emotions,** which seem to be universal experiences. Psychologists distinguish these from **secondary emotions,** which include cultural variations (such as *schadenfreude* or *amaeru*), blends of feelings (the bittersweet emotion of feeling sad and happy at a friend's wedding, say), and degrees of intensity ("fear" can range from nervousness to terror) (J. Russell, 1983). Primary emotions have been identified in several ways: by universally recognized facial expressions; by the existence in most languages of words that label them; and by the predictable appearance of these emotions in child development. Thus the most common emotion words young children use are the basics: *happy, sad, mad,* and *scared.* As they get older, they learn varieties that are specific to their language, such as *ecstatic, depressed, hostile,* or *anxious* (Storm & Storm, 1987).

Depending on how psychologists go about measuring emotions, the list of the "primary" ones varies somewhat. Fear, anger, sadness, joy, surprise, and disgust turn up in most studies. But sometimes laypeople disagree with psychologists. Most Americans consider "love" to be an emotion, even though it doesn't have a typical facial expression (except perhaps the mooning gaze of new sweethearts). In contrast, they don't really think of surprise or disgust as true emotions, although both are registered on the face (Shaver et al., 1987; Storm & Storm, 1987).

---

[4]Excerpts from *Psychology,* 2nd ed., by Carole Wade and Carol Travis.

1. Again, let's analyze it. What is the passage about?

    ____

    ____

    ____

    (Overall, we thought the passage was about how some emotions are found in every culture and how some may vary by culture.)

2. Now, check both sets of annotations. Were there any major differences in the actual information annotated?

    ____

    ____

    ____

    (We tried to annotate just the bare essentials: main concepts, supporting details, and examples.)

3. Were there any major differences in how you annotated as opposed to how we annotated? Did you pull out more or less information than we did?

    ____

    ____

    ____

    ____

If you are like most people learning how to annotate, you probably annotated too much and/or did not put the information in your own words. If you did this, do not be discouraged. Use it as feedback on how to improve. Did the organization that we provided help you figure out what was important? If so, you can see why it is important to put your own organization on your annotations—information will be easier to learn in this form.

Exercise: Annotating Solo

Now take the opportunity to annotate several pages by yourself. Although we show how we annotated the same pages, complete yours before looking at ours. First, read the passage. Then, think about what main points and supporting details are important before you annotate. The last statement is not a misprint. You will not know what is important enough to annotate if you do not read ahead a little. Although it is tempting to annotate each sentence as you read, you will end up writing too much and wasting valuable time. When you annotate, put the information in your own words. Be brief. Use abbreviations, phrases, and symbols, and organize the information with headings and listings. Please start annotating the following passage.

Thinking about Feeling[5]

In the past, many Western philosophers and scientists regarded emotion as the opposite of thinking, and an inferior opposition, at that. "The heart" (emotion) was said to go its own way, in spite of what "the head" (reason) wanted. Some writers believed that following one's heart could be a good thing, as when, say, it led to a happy marriage or a new invention. But most thought that thinking was superior to feeling. Reason, logic, intellectual ideas, judgment, and perception, they said, were better than intuition, hunch, and emotion, just as the mind was supposedly superior to the body and human beings superior to lower animals.

The mind-body battle has been fought in the study of emotions themselves. For centuries, the field has been divided into two traditions. One, the **organic school,** argues that emotions are primarily a matter of biology, of physical events that, like a thumping heart or a giddy blush, are not voluntarily controlled. The other tradition, the **mental school,** argues that emotions are primarily a matter of cognition and perception. Modern researchers are trying to build bridges between mind *and* body, thinking *and* feeling. But the two traditions differ on which comes first.

The organic tradition maintains that feeling comes first and thoughts follow, or are unrelated to emotion. Several lines of evidence support this argument. First, in the development of human beings and our nearest

[5]Excerpts from *Psychology,* 2nd ed., by Carole Wade and Carol Travis.

primate relatives, emotion seems to appear before cognition does: babies weep and show distress at separation long before they understand or perceive reasons for adult behavior; they reveal facial expressions of emotion as mere infants (Stenberg & Campos, 1990). Second, the limbic system, sometimes called the "emotional brain," is involved with emotional expression and behavior, whereas cognitive processes occur in another part of the brain. Third, pure sensory input is enough to stimulate an emotional response, without interference from higher mental processes. Fourth, feeling and thinking are often unrelated. Sometimes people don't know why they feel the way they do, and changing their thoughts doesn't always change their emotional states (Izard, 1984; Zajonc, 1980, 1984).

The mental tradition says that thoughts come first, and this camp also marshalls evidence in its support (Lazarus, 1984). Simple sensory reactions, in this view, cannot properly be called "emotions" at all. Some events will automatically produce reflex actions. If you unexpectedly hear a loud noise, you will show a startle response, but that does not mean you feel "afraid"; the emotion of fear requires the perception of danger. Babies cry and frown to communicate distress, but this doesn't mean they feel "angry." As for brain research, emotions have never been easily assigned to one part of the brain or another. The causes and effects of emotion spread rapidly across both brain hemispheres (Sperry, 1982). The evidence of enormous cultural differences in what produces emotion and in how people respond to emotion means that very little in emotional experience is truly universal or biologically programmed. Finally, new therapies have had great success in treating emotional disorders by changing unrealistic thinking (Beck & Emery, 1985; Lazarus & Folkman, 1984).

The mind-body debate about emotions is a classic case of either-or thinking. There is probably no way to resolve it, because, as we will show, **emotions** consist of three elements: *physiological* changes in the body and face, *cognitive* processes such as interpretations of events, and *cultural* influences that shape the experience and expression of emotion.

When you are done, look at our annotations on pages 60–61 and compare them with your own. It may be helpful to use the checklist on page 59 to guide your review of your annotations. When you compare your annotations with ours, note any of the following:

1. Did you miss any important ideas? How do your annotations compare with ours?

 ____

 ____

 ____

2. Did you copy information word for word, or did you try to put things in your own words where you could? If you copied, why did you copy?

 ____

 ____

 ____

3. Did you have too many details or leave out too many main points?

 ____

 ____

 ____

4. Did you use any symbols (! # & * +/- \ ?)? Which ones?

 ____

 ____

5. If it made sense to do so, did you label or number information in order to organize it?

 ____

 ____

6. The basic test of the quality of your annotations is to cover up the textbook and read your annotations. Do they make sense to you? Will they make sense to you next week or next month? If not, you have not annotated well enough to help you study. You should not have to go back frequently to the actual text to figure out your annotations.

ANNOTATION CHECKLIST

- ☐ My annotations are excellent.
- ☐ I have missed many/some key ideas. I need to go back and annotate them.
- ☐ I need to put my annotations in my own words and try not to copy from the book.
- ☐ I need to be briefer in my annotations.
- ☐ I ignored the graphic aids. I need to go back and annotate them.
- ☐ I need to note the specific examples that could reappear on the exam.
- ☐ I need to number and list the specific facts, characteristics, causes, events, etc., in the margin.
- ☐ My annotations need to focus more on key ideas and less on details.
- ☐ I am annotating too much. It will take me forever to do a chapter!
- ☐ I am underlining rather than annotating. I need to work more on writing my summaries in the margin.
- ☐ I need to develop and use some symbols.
- ☐ I need to develop a method for organizing my annotations.

Adapted from M. L. Simpson and S. L. Nist, "Textbook Annotation: An Effective and Efficient Study Strategy for College Students." *Journal of Reading,* 34, (1990), 122–129. Copyright by the International Reading Association.

Thinking about Feeling[5]

Thinking about Feeling
Long-time debate—mind-body: Which is superior?

In the past, many Western philosophers and scientists regarded emotion as the opposite of thinking, and an inferior opposition, at that. "The heart" (emotion) was said to go its own way, in spite of what "the head" (reason) wanted. Some writers believed that following one's heart could be a good thing, as when, say, it led to a happy marriage or a new invention. But most thought that thinking was superior to feeling. Reason, logic, intellectual ideas, judgment, and perception, they said, were better than intuition, hunch, and emotion, just as the mind was supposedly superior to the body and human beings superior to lower animals.

Same debate in emot.
2 traditions
1) organic school→emots controlled by body; invol.
2) mental school→emots controlled by thought

The mind-body battle has been fought in the study of emotions themselves. For centuries, the field has been divided into two traditions. One, the **organic school,** argues that emotions are primarily a matter of biology, of physical events that, like a thumping heart or a giddy blush, are not voluntarily controlled. The other tradition, the **mental school,** argues that emotions are primarily a matter of cognition and perception. Modern researchers are trying to build bridges between mind *and* body, thinking *and* feeling. But the two traditions differ on which comes first.

ORGANIC
Feeling→thought
Evidence:
1) emot. appears b4 thinking
2) limbic sys. deals w/emot; cogn. occurs elsewhere
3) senses can trigger emot. w/out "higher" thinking

The organic tradition maintains that feeling comes first and thoughts follow, or are unrelated to emotion. Several lines of evidence support this argument. First, in the development of human beings and our nearest primate relatives, emotion seems to appear before cognition does: Babies weep and show distress at separation long before they understand or perceive reasons for adult behavior; they reveal facial expressions of emotion as mere infants (Stenberg & Campos, 1990). Second, the limbic system, sometimes called the "emotional brain," is involved with emotional expression and behavior, whereas cognitive processes occur in another part of the brain. Third, pure sensory input is enough to stimulate an emotional response, without interference from higher

---

[5]Excerpts from *Psychology,* 2nd ed., by Carole Wade and Carol Travis. Copyright © 1989 by Harper & Row, Publishers, Inc., Reprinted by permission of HarperCollins, Inc.

4) emot & thinking can be unrelated

mental processes. Fourth, feeling and thinking are often unrelated. Sometimes people don't know why they feel the way they do, and changing their thoughts doesn't always change their emotional states (Izard, 1984; Zajonc, 1980, 1984).

MENTAL
Thought → feeling
Evidence:
1) sens. reacs aren't "real" emots
2) emots can't easily be located in brain
3) Cultural diffs
4) therapy for emot. probs changes thinking

The mental tradition says that thoughts come first, and this camp also marshalls evidence in its support (Lazarus, 1984). Simple sensory reactions, in this view, cannot properly be called "emotions" at all. Some events will automatically produce reflex actions. If you unexpectedly hear a loud noise, you will show a startle response, but that does not mean you feel "afraid"; the emotion of fear requires the perception of danger. Babies cry and frown to communicate distress, but this doesn't mean they feel "angry." As for brain research, emotions have never been easily assigned to one part of the brain or another. The causes and effects of emotion spread rapidly across both brain hemispheres (Sperry, 1982). The evidence of enormous cultural differences in what produces emotion and in how people respond to emotion means that very little in emotional experience is truly universal or biologically programmed. Finally, new therapies have had great success in treating emotional disorders by changing unrealistic thinking (Beck & Emery, 1985; Lazarus & Folkman, 1984).

Probably not 1 way or the other—must look at relation of the two

emotions
3 elements
1) phys. change
2) cogn. processes
3) cultural influences

The mind-body debate about emotions is a classic case of either-or thinking. There is probably no way to resolve it, because, as we will show, **emotions** consist of three elements: *physiological* changes in the body and face, *cognitive* processes such as interpretations of events, and *cultural* influences that shape the experience and expression of emotion.

What you have been doing while previewing, reading, and annotating this material is monitoring your understanding of the text. Successful students are generally alert and aware while they read and keep tabs on how well they are understanding the material. Try to get in the habit of monitoring your comprehension as you read and study. Ask yourself questions about what and how you are learning. Annotating will help you monitor your understanding paragraph by paragraph.

A word of caution. After you have annotated several pages of your psychology book, you will probably say to yourself, "Forget it! This strategy takes forever! I don't have this kind of time to spend on taking notes!" The strategy does take more effort than simply reading. It's your choice: put in the time necessary to remember and learn so that you will be able to study for the test, or frantically read and reread the night before the test with little chance of remembering or learning the material. Annotation does not cost time; it saves time in the long run.

There is a big difference between reading and studying. First, you read and then you annotate. Next, you take your annotations and do several things with them in order to study and remember.

You can use annotations in many ways to study. We will talk about that in Chapter 7 on studying and Chapter 8 on test preparation. For now, work on becoming a master annotator. Take out your psychology book...preview your assigned chapter...call up what you already know about the topic...divide up the chapter into small, bite-size pieces...and start reading and annotating.

APPLICATION EXERCISES

1. Annotate the chapter(s) you are currently reading in psychology. Analyze your annotations using the checklist on page 59, or ask the instructor, a tutor, or a student who has previously been successful in the class to evaluate your notes.
2. Make a strong effort to annotate all psychology material this quarter/semester. It takes extended practice to become good at this reading strategy. Solicit feedback from instructors or other students.

TERMS TO KNOW

brainstorming
emotions
mental school
organic school
primary emotions
secondary emotions
two-factor theory of emotion

CHAPTER 4

TAKING LECTURE NOTES IN PSYCHOLOGY

GETTING FOCUSED

- *How should you evaluate your current note-taking skills?*
- *How should you prepare to take notes?*
- *How can you take effective lecture notes?*
- *How should you organize your notes for later study?*
- *What are the pros and cons of taping lectures?*

■

Personal Learning Questions

Think about your current method of taking notes from lecture. In what areas of note taking do you have difficulty?

■

Whether you are in a large hall with 400 students or a small classroom with 20 students, one of the main ways you will learn information in psychology is by listening to lectures. In many cases, the information that an instructor offers during a lecture is different from and supplemental to that information that is found in the textbook, and thus you need to be able to take quality notes in order to learn the material and perform well on the tests.

In this chapter, you will evaluate your current note-taking skills, learn a time-tested note-taking method, learn what to listen and watch for in class, and practice with an excerpt from a lecture on dreams. Although the note-taking method might be new to you, the ideas that we are emphasizing in this chapter will not be new: as you have already found in reading, learning vocabulary, studying, and preparing for tests, taking good lecture notes involves active processing on your part. It requires your full attention, and plenty of review.

EVALUATING YOUR CURRENT NOTE-TAKING TECHNIQUES

Take out your psychology notebook, or any course notebook for that matter, if you have not yet taken notes in psychology class. Think about how you get ready to take notes, how you actually take notes in class, and how you use the notes later. Page through your notes and answer the questions in the following checklist on pages 65 and 66 to evaluate your current note-taking skills. The checklist is divided into three main categories: before the lecture, during the lecture, and after the lecture. After you finish reviewing the checklist, we will go through each item in each of the three categories and give you some suggestions for improving your note taking.

LECTURE NOTES EVALUATION CHECKLIST

Circle the response (*yes, sometimes,* or *no*) that best describes your behavior before, during, and after lectures.

Before the Lecture

1.	Do you read the textbook assignment before the topic is lectured on in class?	Yes	Sometimes	No
2.	Do you sit as close to the front of the lecture hall as you can?	Yes	Sometimes	No
3.	Do you come prepared with paper and pens?	Yes	Sometimes	No
4.	Do you use loose-leaf notebook paper?	Yes	Sometimes	No
5.	Do you review your previous notes for a couple of minutes?	Yes	Sometimes	No
6.	Do you have your notebook paper divided into a one-third, two-thirds arrangement?	Yes	Sometimes	No

During the Lecture

1.	Do you sit up straight and lean forward in your chair when taking notes?	Yes	Sometimes	No
2.	Is your handwriting legible?	Yes	Sometimes	No
3.	Do you use just one side of the page?	Yes	Sometimes	No
4.	Do you date your notes?	Yes	Sometimes	No
5.	Do you title your notes?	Yes	Sometimes	No
6.	Do you number the pages?	Yes	Sometimes	No
7.	Do you think before you write?	Yes	Sometimes	No
8.	Do you star or underline important concepts or definitions?	Yes	Sometimes	No
9.	Do you indent details under the main idea?	Yes	Sometimes	No
10.	Do you leave plenty of space between main ideas on a page?	Yes	Sometimes	No
11.	Do you use abbreviations, phrases, and/or symbols?	Yes	Sometimes	No
12.	Do you write down information that the instructor writes on the board or overhead?	Yes	Sometimes	No
13.	Do you listen for cues in the instructor's manner of presentation, like volume, speed, and repetition?	Yes	Sometimes	No

(continues)

Lecture Notes Evaluation Checklist (continued)

14.	Do you listen for "signal words" in the instructor's lecture?	Yes	Sometimes	No
15.	Do you write down the answers to questions other students ask during the lecture?	Yes	Sometimes	No
	After the Lecture			
1.	Do you review your notes within 24 hours of the lecture?	Yes	Sometimes	No
2.	Do you rewrite your notes?	Yes	Sometimes	No
3.	Do you fill in missing information and write out information that you abbreviated if necessary?	Yes	Sometimes	No
4.	Do you "annotate" your notes, or write questions about them in the left margin?	Yes	Sometimes	No
5.	Do you rehearse your notes before you start intense studying for the test?	Yes	Sometimes	No

Before the Lecture

A note-taking strategy begins before you ever put pen to paper. You can do several things before the lecture that will prepare you to take notes efficiently and effectively.

1. *Read the assignment.* If your syllabus or instructor has indicated that today's lecture will be on dreams, it is a good idea to have read that section in your textbook beforehand. Then you will have your own schema operating as you listen to the lecture. This means that you will know what you do and do not understand, and you can listen for additional information, answers to questions you may have had during reading, and clarification of important points in the textbook. If you have not read the assignment, you will not have a framework in place for the information you are about to hear in the lecture. You will be more likely to write down everything the instructor says because you do not know what is and is not important.

   Conversely, if you are not yet skilled at note taking, you may not write down everything you need to, and you will have to rely on memory. This means you will lose 80% of the lecture, because we only remember approximately 20% of what we hear. There is another important reason for reading the assignment before the lecture. If you wait to read the assignment until after the lecture, it may then be too late to ask questions and get clarification from the instructor because he or she has moved on to another topic in the next lecture.

2. *Sit close to the front.* When you sit in the back of a large lecture hall, people and things in the rows in front of you steal your attention away from the lecture. If you sit close to the front of the lecture hall or classroom, you will have fewer distractions from your note-taking duties. Also, when you're closer to the action, you tend to become more interested in the lecture. You are also more likely to ask questions when you can see the instructor's face, catch his or her attention, and not have to shout to be heard. Another good reason for sitting up front is that the instructor may get to know you better or at least begin to recognize your face. When an instructor recognizes you and sees your interest and attention in the lectures, it may make a difference when grades are assigned.

3. *Come prepared.* We all forget things sometimes. However, if you frequently forget to bring paper and pens to a lecture, you probably are having an organization problem, and success in class may not be the first thing on your mind. Come prepared to take good notes and do well: have your notebook stocked with paper and pens. Remember to bring an extra pen in case one runs out of ink.

4. *Use loose-leaf notebook paper.* Use paper that you can place in a three-ring notebook. This makes it easier to arrange your notes by topic if necessary. Loose-leaf paper is also neater than paper ripped out of a spiral notebook, and you will feel more organized if your notes are neat.

5. *Review your notes at the beginning of class.* After you find your seat, take a couple of minutes to review your notes from the last time you attended psychology class. This brief review will orient you to the note taking task at hand.

6. *Draw a vertical line one-third of the way across the page from the left.* If you can find it in your campus bookstore, buy paper lined in this way (See Figure 4.1.). This paper is set up for using the Cornell method of note taking.[1] (This method will be described in detail later in the chapter.)

---

[1]W. Pauk, *How to Study in College* (Boston: Houghton Mifflin, 1984).

Figure 4.1 The Cornell Method Format

During the Lecture

Start taking notes at the very beginning of class. Often, the instructor gives you important information regarding homework or other assignments at this time, or indicates what the topic for the day's lecture will be. Be alert from the beginning.

1. *Sit up and lean forward.* If you slouch in your chair with your legs over the seat in front of you, you are more prepared to watch a movie, perhaps, than you are to pay attention and take good lecture notes. Sitting up straight and leaning slightly forward will help you concentrate, pay attention, become involved in the lecture, and listen better. Your body position can affect your mind, and sitting up and leaning forward signals your mind that it's time for business.

2. *Write legibly.* You may think that as long as you can read your writing, it does not matter if anyone else can. To some extent, that's true. But you will find it easier to study later if your notes are written clearly. You will also feel more organized. Besides, you won't have time when you study to puzzle over scribbles and hieroglyphics. If you can't help but be sloppy when you take notes in class, you may want to invest time in rewriting or word processing your notes each evening after class.

3. *Use only one side of the page.* Although it may seem like a waste of paper, using just one side of the page will allow you to use the reverse side for questions and notes you may want to make based on later lectures or the related reading assignment. Also, the extra space contributes to a feeling of organization and neatness.

4, 5, 6. *Date, title, and number your notes.* Dating, titling, and numbering each page of your notes will prove invaluable if you lose any pages or if you need to get notes from a class you missed. Also, titling your notes helps to organize them for later studying.

7. *Think before you write.* Many students make the mistake of trying to write down every word the instructor says, fearing that they will miss something crucially important. In most cases, you will take better notes if you listen to what the instructor says, think about it, and then decide what to write. Taking notes from lecture is very similar to annotating a reading assignment. First, you read a paragraph or section; next, you think about what is important to know and what is not; and finally, you write the important information and supporting details. The same principles apply to lectures: listen to the main concept being discussed; think about what is important to know about that concept, if anything; then, write down the essential information. Paying close attention and reading the textbook assignment before the

lecture will put you in a good position to evaluate what you need to write down from the lecture. If you just write everything the instructor says, you are not likely to be concentrating on the content of the lecture, and your notes will not make a lot of sense to you later.

Sometimes, however, you do want to write down nearly everything the instructor says. If you know absolutely nothing about a topic or are very confused by it, you will want to write down everything you can so that you can go over your notes that evening and try to make sense of the information.

8. *Star or underline important main concepts.* Make sure that the main points of a lecture stand out in your notes, whether that means starring them, underlining them, or just leaving lots of white space before and after them. When you study your notes later, you want to be able to focus on the main points. Here is where you may want to use a highlighter. Highlight the information you predict will be on the test.

9. *Indent details under the main idea.* If all your notes are organized on the page so that main ideas and details are indistinguishable, your studying is much more difficult than it needs to be.

10. *Leave blank space between main ideas.* After finishing with the details under a main idea, leave a line or two blank before starting with the next main idea flush left against the margin. This format aids organization and makes studying easier later.

11. *Use your own shorthand.* Although we do not expect you to take shorthand as a secretary might, you should begin to develop your own ways of abbreviating, using symbols, and otherwise cutting down on the amount of writing you need to do in class.

    For example, don't bother writing articles like *a, and, the, these, this,* and other short words. (See Table 4.1 for suggested symbols and abbreviations.) Using certain abbreviations and shorthand frequently becomes second nature, and you will find yourself using these same abbreviations for years.

12. *Write what the instructor writes on the chalkboard or overhead.* Generally, if the instructor goes to the trouble of writing something on the board or overhead, it is worth your attention. New

terminology, definitions, graphs, charts, maps, and so on, are important and should be copied exactly.

13. *Listen for the instructor's cues in manner of presentation.* Consciously or unconsciously, many instructors increase the loudness of their voices, slow down, and/or repeat words when they think they are delivering especially important information. Be alert to these cues in lectures.

14. *Listen for "signal words."* Signal words are verbal cues that alert you to important information, such as "most important," "least," "there are several causes of," "there are three theories that," "the greatest number of," "the fewest," "first," "next," "finally," "in addition," "for example," "be sure to know," "the main difference/similarity," and so on. These signals will give you clues about what is important to know as well as how to organize your notes for easier studying later.

15. *Write down other students' questions.* Evaluate other students' questions for possibly important information. Write down those questions and answers that you deem worthwhile. Sometimes, someone else's question leads the instructor to elaborate on an important or confusing point, and the explanation may be helpful to you.

You might want to write down these guidelines for taking notes and bring the list to class to refer to as you take notes. With practice, you will almost automatically remember what to take notes on during lectures.

After the Lecture

Taking the time to review, rewrite, "fix," annotate, and rehearse your notes soon after the lecture will dramatically increase your retention of the material.

1. *Review your notes within 24 hours of the lecture.* Taking the time to review your notes for 5–10 minutes within 24 hours of the lecture will increase by 50% your retention of the material. That's a lot of payback for very little initial effort. It will also give you plenty of time to get help with any material that you may have found confusing.

2. *Rewrite your notes only if they are hard to read.* If you are taking a full course load, you probably do not have time to rewrite your

TABLE 4.1 SUGGESTED SYMBOLS AND ABBREVIATIONS

WORD	STANDARD SYMBOLS
and	&
therefore, so	∴
with	w/
without	w/o
same as, equal to	=
not the same as, not equal to	≠
greater than	>
less than	<

WORD	ABBREVIATIONS
You can delete vowels from many words, and otherwise shorten words, without confusing yourself. Below are some examples of psychology words you will write frequently that can be written in "shorthand":	
learning	lrng
social learning	soc lrng
psychology	psych
behavioral	behavl
cognitive	cogn
independent and dependent variables	IV, DV
correlation	corr
experiment	exp
central nervous system	CNS
conscious	CS
consciousness	CSS
perception	percep
classical conditioning	CC
operant conditioning	OC
reinforcement	reinf
short-term and long-term memory	STM, LTM
emotion	emot
motivation	motiv
extrinsic and intrinsic motivation	EM, IM
development	dev

notes. Try to do the job well at the time of lecture. However, if the material is very difficult and/or if your handwriting is nearly illegible, it is probably worth taking the time to rewrite your notes.

3. *Fill in missing information.* During your 5–10 minutes of review, fill in any important words you may have missed during the lecture. If your abbreviations confuse you, you may want to write out the full spelling of the word now before you forget what your abbreviations stood for.

4. *Annotate your notes in the left margin.* After the lecture, use the left margin (see Figure 4.1) for one of two purposes. You can annotate your notes and just pull out the labels for the main concepts, or you can pose questions about the material. Either way, you will use the material in the left margin later to test yourself on the information. (See the description of the Cornell method that follows).

5. *Rehearse your notes long before the test.* During your review, rehearse the main ideas and supporting details out loud. If you start rehearsing immediately, before a test is on the horizon, your study time later will be greatly reduced, and you will be more likely to remember the information.

▪

PERSONAL LEARNING QUESTIONS

Do you typically ignore your notes until it's time to study for the test? How can you make time in your schedule to rewrite and review your notes as soon as possible after taking them?

▪

Taping

Students often wonder if it is worthwhile to tape lectures and transcribe them later to ensure that they do not miss any important information. In our experience both as students and as instructors, we have found that taping is generally a waste of time. You simply do not have the time to listen to the tape and to keep rewinding it to get every last word down on paper. You end up spending nearly three times as much time on the class as you would if you had just concentrated and taken good notes during the lecture.

A situation in which you might benefit from taping a lecture is when the instructor has a heavy foreign accent, and you need time to figure out what he or she is saying. Other situations include if the course is so difficult that you are completely lost or if the instructor speaks so rapidly that you can't follow what he or she is saying (you could also try politely asking the instructor to speak more slowly). If you do decide that you would like to tape a lecture, however, first ask the instructor for permission to do so.

Now that you have evaluated your current note-taking skills and gotten some advice on the subject, you can better appreciate the note-taking method that we are about to introduce.

CORNELL NOTE-TAKING METHOD

The Cornell method of note taking is probably the most effective note taking strategy that we know. Research has proven its effectiveness, and students attest to finding the strategy very helpful. The method incorporates most of the suggestions that we have already given you in the previous few pages, so we are now going to focus on the actual organization and format of your notes using the Cornell method.

1. It is time for some practice. Take a sheet of paper and draw a line down the page one-third of the way over from the left edge, as in Figure 4.1. (You can also purchase tablets of paper already ruled in this way.) Take notes only on the right two-thirds of the page, leaving the left margin for annotations or questions later. Write the date at the top of the page, and number the page.

2. Below is a short excerpt from a lecture on dreams by one of the authors of this book. If possible, ask a roommate or family member to take the role of an instructor and read this lecture. Take notes as you would if you were sitting in a large lecture hall. Keep our "During the Lecture" suggestions in mind as you take notes.

3. Before using the left-hand margin, compare your notes with ours in Example 4.1 on page 76. How do your notes differ? Students new at taking notes in college tend to write either everything or not nearly enough, and they tend not to structure their notes clearly and neatly. We used abbreviations and left out unimportant words; we numbered the list of possible reasons why we

dream; we dated, titled, and numbered the notes; and we wrote legibly. Now, when we review the notes, we can read them easily, and they are organized for more effective study.

4. Now is the time to use the left margin. As we mentioned earlier, this margin is used for annotations or questions about the notes that will help you study later. In Example 4.2 on pages 76–77, we used our left margin for a combination of annotations and questions. When we study these notes later, we can cover the lecture notes, ask ourselves these questions about the material, and try to recite the answers. We briefly annotated the theories about the purposes of dreaming with key words to jog our memory. Practice annotating pages from your notes and writing questions on other pages to see which approach or combination of approaches works best for you.

Exercise: Sample Lecture

Why do we dream? No one knows for sure why we dream, although we do know that dreaming—not just sleep, but dreaming—is necessary for normal functioning. Experiments have been done in which people are allowed to get 8 hours of sleep, but whenever they begin to dream (this can be determined by monitoring their brainwaves with an EEG—**electroencephalograph**), the experimenter awakens them. As soon as they are awake, they are allowed to go back to sleep. When subjects were kept from dreaming in this way, they began to **hallucinate** during their waking hours. The hallucinations only stopped after subjects were allowed to get a night's sleep that included dreaming.

So, we need to dream, but why? What purpose does it serve? There are a number of theories. Freud believed that dreaming is a way to safely express fears and desires that are bottled up (**repressed**) inside us. We cannot consciously acknowledge these forbidden fears and desires (which mostly involve sex and violence), so they are expressed in dreams. Even in dreams, however, some of the material is too uncomfortable for us, so these fears and desires are often disguised using symbols. This is why dreams are often confusing and disjointed.

Other theories of the function of dreams are more mundane. One possibility is that we dream in order to make sense of the day's experiences. Dreams are thus a working through of the things that have happened to us that day, along with an attempt to fit these experiences into our past experiences.

A third possibility is that dreams are a way for us to "throw out" useless experiences that have occurred that day. In this case, as in the previous theory, we are sorting through the day's events, but not to store them away. Rather, we dispose of what is not useful to us.

A fourth possibility is that dreams serve as "play time" for our unconscious mind. Perhaps the unconscious mind needs a chance each day to be in control and engage in recreation of a sort.

Finally, it is possible that dreams serve more than one purpose. Often, we think that there must be one explanation and one explanation only for some phenomenon. But we are very complex, and it may be that a number of the theories reflect functions that dreams serve. At this point, we don't know for sure.

EXAMPLE 4.1

3/23

Dreams

Why do we dream? Not sure, but it's necess. for normal functioning. S's in exp. were kept from drmg → hallucinated (can tell if drmg by EEG—monitors brain waves.)

Theories about why we dream:

1) Freud—drms are way to express fears/desires that we <u>repress.</u> May come out in <u>symbols</u> if the fears/desires are too wild for us to deal w/. Why drms are confusing.
2) Make sense of day's events. Work thru them to store.
3) Throw out useless events from day (not store).
4) "Play time" for UCS.
5) More than 1 of the above may be correct. Complex.

Psychs—unsure what purpose drms serve.

EXAMPLE 4.2

	3/23
	Dreams
Why dream?	Why do we dream? Not sure, but it's necess. for normal functioning. S's in exp. were kept from drmg→ hallucinated (can tell if drmg by EEG — monitors brain waves.)
What happens if we're kept from drmg?	
Theories?	Theories about why we dream:
1) Freud	1) Freud—drms are way to express fears/desires that we repress. May come out in symbols if the fears/desires are too wild for us to deal w/. Why drms are confusing.
2) make sense	2) Make sense of day's events. Work thru them to store.
3) throw out	3) Throw out useless events from day (not store).
4) play time	4) "Play time" for UCS.
5) more than 1	5) More than 1 of the above may be correct. Complex.
Who knows?!	Psychs—unsure what purpose drms serve.

The keys to learning the information in your notes are the same as they are for learning information from your textbook: active processing, attention, and plenty of rehearsal.

Go See the Instructor During Office Hours

A final word of advice: if you have any questions about the lecture or reading assignments, or if you want to know more about a topic discussed in class, go visit the instructor. You are likely to get considerable insight into an issue or question. When you are one of three or four hundred students, it is difficult to get individualized attention to your questions in class. Most instructors, however, enjoy having students visit them during office hours. They are experts and want to share their knowledge, debate topics, and listen to your ideas. Also, your instructor will be more likely to remember you if you show your sincere interest. Such attention may prompt you to become more involved in class, and it may help you if you have a borderline grade.

APPLICATION EXERCISES

1. Try different seats in your classroom or lecture hall over a week. Notice how different locations influence your experience of the class, attention level, willingness to participate, and interest.
2. Work with a study partner or group on improving your notes. Have each of your partners complete the "Lecture Notes Evaluation Checklist" at the beginning of this chapter. Commit to helping each other improve note-taking skills. Evaluate each other's notes after each lecture or a week's worth of lectures. Continue until you feel proficient in note taking.
3. If you are skeptical about the effectiveness of this note-taking method, try it in your psychology class and continue taking notes in your usual way in another class. Compare the effectiveness of each method after half the term.

TERMS TO KNOW

electroencephalograph
hallucinate
repressed

CHAPTER 5

THE LANGUAGE OF PSYCHOLOGY

GETTING FOCUSED

- *How do you recognize the concepts of psychology?*
- *Have you learned the technical language of psychology?*
- *How do you identify important terms to study?*
- *What strategies can you develop to learn psychology vocabulary?*

▪

PERSONAL LEARNING QUESTIONS

What do you already know about learning technical vocabulary? How have you learned new concepts in your previous courses? Does learning vocabulary present you with any particular problems?

▪

> ***jargon*** *1 a: confused unintelligible language b: a strange, outlandish, or barbarous language or dialect 2: the technical terminology or characteristic idiom of a special activity or group 3: obscure and often pretentious language marked by circumlocutions and long words*

While you are wading through your psychology text, you may be tempted to define "jargon" using definition 1 or 3, or some combination of the two. But the second definition is the right one for our purposes in this chapter. Psychology, like every specialized field, has its own peculiar way of saying things. In this chapter, we will discuss why it is important to learn psychology's vocabulary, what it means to really know a concept, how to figure out what words to learn, ways of understanding the important words, and strategies for studying vocabulary.

CONCEPTS

It is not enough to memorize the definitions of words. For the words to be useful to you, you have to learn the **concepts.** Concepts are the general, abstract ideas behind the words. The concepts help you understand the "big picture." It usually takes more than a one sentence definition to understand a concept, so the one-sentence definitions provided in glossaries can often be deceptive or incomplete.

For example, before you read your psychology textbook, you may think of the term **memory** as meaning "remembering information." Your textbook may provide a one-sentence definition, such as "the capacity to retain and retrieve information." Usually there is a whole chapter on memory that describes memory systems, the processes in each system, how we think information is encoded, stored, and retrieved, different theories about how memory works, why forgetting occurs, the biology of memory, and more. So, memory cannot really be reduced to a simple one-sentence definition because it involves many complex concepts.

Range of Conceptual Knowledge

Let's take another look at the memory example in the last paragraph. Notice how you can have a range of knowledge about a concept.[1] You can have a vague, fuzzy idea about what memory is ("remembering information"), then a more specific understanding ("the capacity to retain and retrieve information"), and a fuller understanding yet (what you know after reading the whole chapter on memory). A psychologist who only studies memory has an even more complete knowledge about the subject. As you can see, it is not a matter of knowing everything or nothing. You can start with very little knowledge about something and then expand your schema for it a great deal.

Another way of looking at this range of knowledge is to think about what you already know about a word that you come across when you read. If you read the word **narcissism,** for example, your knowledge of the meaning of the concept could fall into one of four categories: (1) you are totally lost—you have never seen or heard of the word before; (2) you think you have seen or heard of it, but you do not know what it means, and you would not use it in casual conversation; (3) you know you have seen or heard of it, you have a vague idea of its meaning, and you might use it in a sentence; or (4) you can use the word accurately. (By the way, narcissism is the state of having an exaggerated sense of vanity and self-importance.)

It is important to understand the concepts in psychology, but it is also important to be conscious of exactly what you do and do not know, and to pay attention to how you learn things best. The more you know about your own strengths and weaknesses as a student and about the knowledge you have about different topics, the better off you will be. You can determine what strategies work best for you and what strategies to try when you are having problems.

---

[1]P. Drum, "Vocabulary Knowledge," in *Searches for Meaning in Reading/Learning Processes and Instruction,* ed. J. A. Niles and L. A. Harris (Rochester, NY: National Reading Conference, 1983), pp. 163–171.

GENERAL AND TECHNICAL VOCABULARY

Vocabulary in textbooks comes in two varieties: general and technical. General words are used everywhere, from textbooks to comic books; they are not related to a particular subject area. Words like *neighborhood* and *odor* are general words. Sometimes, you may come across general words that you have never heard of before, but once you hear the definition, you realize that you already know the concept and have other words for it. For example, you may read the word *indigent*. You have never seen it before, but find out that it means "extremely poor; impoverished." You know what "extremely poor" means, so you now know what *indigent* means as well.

It is important to pay attention to unfamiliar general words. A larger vocabulary makes you a better writer, a better reader, and a better thinker. Those first two advantages of a large vocabulary are self-explanatory, but you may want a little elaboration on the third. For the most part, we think in words. Generally, then, you can only think of things for which you have words. If you have more words to use, you can think better.

Technical words are words that apply to a particular subject, like **pheromone** (a chemical substance released by an organism that affects the physical structure and behavior of other similar organisms) and **circadian rhythm** (the body's biological rhythm over a 24-hour period). You may have never heard of these words before, and the concepts may be unfamiliar. This situation is the toughest because you are starting from nothing to create a schema for each concept.

With psychology terminology, you will see words that look like general words that you have seen before, but the meaning is different, or more specific and technical. This situation is tricky because whenever you see the word in its psychological context, you have to deliberately think of the word differently than you are used to, or else you will get confused. For example, you may think that **projection** means how a film is shown on a movie screen, but in psychology, it refers to a defense mechanism in which a person's unacceptable feelings and thoughts are attributed to (projected onto) someone else. **Ego** is another example. We often talk about someone as "having a big ego" or suggest that people "let their egos get in the way." In this context, we use ego to mean something closer to "pride." In psychology, the ego is the part of us of which we are consciously aware. What you think of as "you" is your ego, according to psychology. Focusing on intended meanings helps avoid confusion. In the psychology material you are currently reading, pay attention to the general words you do not know; the general words that have specific, technical meanings in psychology; and the new technical words with which you are unfamiliar.

Figuring Out Which Words to Learn

A textbook usually alerts you to the most important words by putting them in boldface print or italics or by printing the word and a definition in the margin of the text. Good textbooks will also provide you with a definition of a word in the text where the word first occurs. But this definition usually consists of one sentence that will not be very helpful until you keep reading and learn how the word fits into the big picture. For example, you may be reading along and come across the following information:

> *When a response is first acquired, learning is usually most rapid if the response is reinforced each time it occurs. This procedure of reinforcing every response is called* continuous reinforcement.[2]

Then, out in the margin, you see:

> continuous reinforcement: *a reinforcement schedule in which a particular response is always reinforced.*

If you have not yet learned about operant conditioning, this definition is probably gibberish to you. Even if you have already learned about operant conditioning, if you do not understand the bigger concepts of operant conditioning and reinforcement and how continuous reinforcement fits into the bigger picture, it does not help to memorize the definition of continuous reinforcement. If you were to memorize each definition as if it were an isolated piece of information, you would be confused and frustrated by a test question like this one:

> *A researcher puts a cat in a room. There is a sprinkler on in the room, so it seems like it is raining to the cat. The cat is not pleased. The cat learns that sometimes when it presses a lever with its paw,*

---

[2]Excerpts from *Psychology,* 2nd ed., by Carole Wade and Carol Travis. Copyright © 1989 by Harper & Row, Publishers, Inc., Reprinted by permission of HarperCollins, Inc.

the rain stops for a few minutes. The cat spends a great deal of time pressing the lever. This is an example of learning through:

a. intermittent positive reinforcement.
b. intermittent negative reinforcement.
c. continuous positive reinforcement.
d. continuous negative reinforcement.

Questions like these are common. Not only do you have to know the difference between **continuous** and **intermittent reinforcement,** but you have to tie that in to a knowledge of the difference between **positive** and **negative reinforcement.** (By the way, the correct answer is b).

The point is: pay attention to the words that the textbook highlights, but try to relate the little pieces (the definitions of individual concepts) to the big picture.

▪

PERSONAL LEARNING QUESTIONS

In the psychology chapter you are currently reading, pull out the main concepts that are emphasized and ask yourself how these concepts relate to each other. Explain the relationships aloud to a study partner or write it down to make sense of the information.

▪

What to Do If Key Words Are Not Identified

If key words are not highlighted in the text, there are a few strategies that will help you figure out most of the words you need to know.

Begin by turning to the back of your textbook and looking in the glossary to see if the author thought the word was important enough to list and define. If it is not there, consider the following: Did the instructor say anything at the beginning of the semester or quarter about what terms you should learn? Will tests focus on vocabulary found mostly in the book, in lectures, or both? Is the word repeated often in the chapter or book and/or used frequently in lecture? Decide if you will need to understand it.

Another difficult situation is when the author uses technical terms in the text, and they are not the most important terms to know, but in order to understand what he or she is talking about, you have to figure out what those words mean. The author may wrongly assume you know what these words mean. For example, if you are reading the "Emotions" chapter in your psychology book, you might come across this paragraph:

> *Psychologists in the organic tradition have long sought to identify specific areas in the brain that might be responsible for emotions. Some researchers have traced emotion to the limbic system and hypothalamus, evolutionarily old parts of the brain that human beings share with other species.*[3]

If your instructor skipped the "Brain" chapter or has not assigned it yet, this passage may not make sense to you. It is not that this section is poorly written; it is just that you may not yet have enough background knowledge to understand this paragraph, and you are going to have to refer to the brain chapter for help.

Of course, some books are poorly written, and your knowledge or lack of it is not the issue. In this case, it might be wise to check out another introductory psychology book from the library and use it to interpret the one your instructor picked. This may be less time consuming than struggling with a confusing textbook.

▪

PERSONAL LEARNING QUESTIONS

Does your textbook provide you with enough information to understand the concepts presented?

▪

Strategies for Understanding Important Words

There are a few ways that you can try to figure out the meanings of words that you think you need to know. These ways are probably familiar to you, but we want to address them and point out their advantages and disadvantages. Your choices for figuring out what words mean are: using dictionaries, glossaries, context clues, and structural analysis; asking the instructor; and simply learning new vocabulary by reading more.

Dictionaries Using the dictionary to learn meanings of unknown words can be frustrating. Why? A dictionary is an alphabetical list of words,

[3]Excerpts from *Psychology,* 2nd ed., by Carole Wade and Carol Travis. Copyright © 1989 by Harper & Row, Publishers, Inc., Reprinted by permission of HarperCollins, Inc.

isolated from the context in which those words occur, and often it has several meanings for each word. These meanings may be radically different or, at the other extreme, just slightly different from each other. If you have some experience with the word that is being defined in your textbook and are looking for a little clarification, a dictionary can help. You usually use a dictionary to find the meaning of a word that you do not have experience with! Frequently you are left practically where you started, lost and confused, especially if you pick the wrong definition.

Our advice is: if the word you do not know appears to be general, try the dictionary and use context clues and structural analysis (see subsequent paragraphs) to help you choose the appropriate definition. If the word is technical, you are probably better off using the glossary in the back of the textbook, because the author or publisher chose the most appropriate definition for the word as it is used in the text.

Glossaries The glossary in your textbook is a good place to look to figure out what a word means. You do not have to wade through several definitions and try to pick the best one; it has already been done for you. Use the glossary to determine if the word is important to know and to get its precise definition.

Do not try to memorize the exact words used in the glossary definition. Instead, try to focus less on memorizing a set of words and more on understanding the concept behind the definition.

Context Clues Context clues are how most people try to figure out a word's meaning. You use the context of the sentence or paragraph in which the unfamiliar word occurs. This technique consists of rereading the sentence with the word in it, going back and reading the previous sentences, and reading ahead to see if you can get a clue in later sentences. Sometimes it works, and sometimes it does not. If a definition is not explicitly provided, you have to piece one together from the feelings you get about the words or how they are used. For example, you may read, "Skinner and the behaviorists were vocal in denouncing as repugnant the idea that psychology is first and foremost the study of the workings of the mind." If you do not know what *repugnant* means, you can get a good idea just by looking at the context in which the word is found. In this example, it is clear that Skinner and the behaviorists (sounds like a rock group) did not like the idea, because they denounced it. What kind of feeling do you get from the word *repugnant?* It sounds negative, doesn't it? It sounds like something disgusting, which is precisely what the word means.

If the word is important and context does not help much, go to the glossary or dictionary. If you decide that the word is not very important, move on. Be prepared to be wrong sometimes, but part of being a good student is making decisions about what information is most important to learn and being right most of the time. You cannot learn everything instantly. Permit yourself to be selective.

Structural Analysis Structural analysis means looking at the structure of the word to try to get a clue to its meaning. You probably remember this technique from English class. You examine the word for a familiar prefix, root, or suffix. Structural analysis usually works best in the physical and biological sciences. You can "pull apart" words like *cytoplasm, microscope,* and *arthropod* pretty easily. But it can sometimes work in psychology as well.

You probably have seen lists of prefixes and roots before. Rather than memorizing these lists, one of the best ways to learn to use structural analysis is to think of words that you do know that have the same prefixes and roots as the word you do not know, and work from there. For example, you know what *cognition* and *recognition* mean. Notice that *cognition* and *recognition* are the same word, except for the *re-*. The root they have in common is *cogn*. Any guess about its meaning? *Cogn* means "know," which makes sense if you think about the words. Cognition is thinking, or trying to know something. Recognition is seeing something and realizing that you have known it before, or in other words "knowing again." If you peek ahead to the list that we have given you, you will see that *re-* means "again," so *recognition* literally means "again knowing."

This technique works well for some people, and if you are one of them, Table 5.1 lists some of the common prefixes and root words that show up in a lot of psychology terms. This list is not exhaustive, but it should give you a good starting point (or at least a good source to which you can refer). Do not try to simply memorize the prefixes and roots, because their definitions will not be meaningful in isolation. Use examples of words you know to remind you of the meanings.

Ask Your Instructor Your psychology instructor is probably the closest expert in psychology to whom you have access. She or he is the best person to ask what a particular word means and which concepts are important to know. If you do not understand a word and want clarification, just ask your instructor before or after class, or stop by during her or his office hours. Helping you learn is a large part of an instructor's job, and she or he should be more than happy to help you.

TABLE 5.1 COMMON PREFIXES AND ROOT WORDS IN PSYCHOLOGY TERMINOLOGY

PREFIX OR ROOT	MEANING	EXAMPLE
anti	**against**	*antidepressant drugs*—drugs that work against depression *antisocial personality disorder*—disorder where the person goes against the acceptable behaviors of society and does not care
bio	**life**	*biofeedback*—a technique for controlling bodily functions (life functions) by attending to an instrument that monitors the function and signals changes in it *biology*—the study of life
cogn	**know**	*cognition*—the act or process of knowing *recognition*—the ability to identify previously encountered material (to know again)
de	**do the opposite of; remove**	*deindividuation*—in groups or crowds, the loss of awareness of one's own individuality *depersonalization*—the loss of one's individuality and humanity
ego	**self**	*ego*—the part of our mind that thinks conscious thoughts; what we usually think of as most truly "us" *egocentric*—unable to take other people's perspectives; self-centered *egotistical*—believing one is superior to others
homeo	**same**	*homeostasis*—same state
mnem, memor, mem	**memory**	*mnemonic device*—a technique for improving memory *amnesia*—loss of memory
neuro	**nerve**	*neurotransmitter*—chemical substance released by a neuron at the synapse that transmits information to the receiving neuron *neuropsychology*—the field of psychology that studies the neural and biochemical bases of behavior and mental processes *neurosis*—a mild psychological disorder, a nervous disorder
path	**disease**	*pathology* (pathological)—(relating to) the study of disease *pathogenic*—causing disease or suffering
phob	**fear**	*phobia*—an irrational fear *hydrophobia*—fear of water

physio	**physical**	*physiology*—study of the functions and activities of living matter and of the physical and chemical phenomena involved
psycho	**mind**	*psychology*—science of mind and behavior *psychiatry*—a branch of medicine that deals with mental, emotional, or behavioral disorders *psychometrics*—measurement of mental abilities and traits *psychotherapist*—person who treats mental or emotional disorders *psychoanalyst*—person who treats mental or emotional disorders using the techniques developed by Freud *psychosomatic*—the interaction between a physical illness or condition and psychological states
re	**again**	*recognize*—to know again *replicate*—to duplicate or repeat *reinforcement*—the process by which a stimulus or event strengthens or increases the probability of the response that follows (the response will happen again) *regression*—a defense mechanism in which a person returns to an earlier stage of development, behaving in immature ways
retro	**backward**	*retroactive interference*—forgetting that occurs when recently learned material interferes with the ability to remember similar material stored previously *retrograde amnesia*—loss of the ability to remember events or experiences that occurred before some particular time
socio	**social**	*social psychology*—the field of psychology that studies individuals in a social context *sociobiology*—a school of thought that attempts to account for social behavior in terms of genetics and evolution *sociocultural perspective*—social and cultural influences on behavior
soma, somato	**body**	*psychosomatic*—relating to the interaction between a physical illness or condition and psychological states *somatoform disorders*—physical disorders that have no demonstrable medical cause
sub	**under, below**	*subconscious*—mental activities below the threshold of conscious awareness *subliminal*—information that enters the mind below the level of conscious awareness

If you go to your instructor to find out whether a concept is important to know, avoid giving the impression that you only want to know if it is going to be on the test. Most instructors interpret this to mean, "I'm not interested in this course, so I'm only going to learn what I absolutely have to." Although you may not feel this way at all, carefully watch how you phrase your question. For example, you may be confused by the many terms describing different abnormal sexual behaviors. Instead of asking your instructor, "Do we have to know what **voyeur** means for the test?", you will get more helpful and complete information by asking something like, "This textbook gives a lot of examples of deviant sexual behavior, but there's not much detail about each one. Should we focus on **deviance** in general rather than all the examples of it?" This kind of question will probably prompt your instructor to give you an informative answer that will help you understand the material better and prepare for the test more effectively.

Read More The best, most effective way to learn both general and technical vocabulary is to read... a lot. People with the largest vocabularies are those who are voracious readers and writers. When you read a lot, you see the same words over and over in different contexts, so you develop fuller meanings for those words. You start to use them in your own conversation and writing. Also, you are always coming across new words, so you are continually expanding your vocabulary.

If you have not been an avid reader, do not worry. There is no critical time in your life that you have to start reading in order to gain the benefits. The more you read, the larger your vocabulary, the better you will write, the faster you will read, the better you will think, and the more you will want to read. Our society gives the advantage to the literate and the articulate. We are not suggesting that you go out and pick up a volume of *The Complete Works of Shakespeare* if you dislike Shakespeare. Begin by reading things you enjoy. Read Stephen King, magazines, newspapers, romances, cereal boxes, or anything.

Try each of these strategies for understanding vocabulary in your psychology course this semester or quarter to determine which ones work best for you. Remember that you usually need more than one strategy to meet the demands of the many different learning situations you encounter.

STRATEGIES FOR STUDYING PSYCHOLOGY TERMINOLOGY

We have already discussed how to figure out definitions and which psychological concepts are important to learn. We have also mentioned repeatedly that you should not memorize one definition after another, but instead, learn the words in context and keep the big picture in mind. Now, we are going to give you some suggestions for remembering these terms once you understand what they mean. As we discussed in Chapter 3, learning is more effective when you actively process the information. Do something with the material, such as reorganizing it or relating it to a personal experience. Here are some strategies for learning psychology jargon that help you actively process the information.

Imagery

One of the best things you can do with material that you want to remember is make some sort of mental picture or image of it. For example, throughout the rest of this book, we are going to give you an arsenal of "weapons" to use when you are studying. Picture yourself walking to your next test, armed to the teeth. You are carrying Rambo-like machine guns in each hand and extra bullets strapped across your chest. This is an overly dramatic image, but that is exactly how it should be if you want to remember it.

Let's look at another example, one that is more closely related to learning in psychology. Let's say you want to remember that the **cerebellum** is the part of the brain that controls bodily balance and coordination. First, you have to come up with a way to remember *cerebellum,* a word that does not automatically leap into long-term memory. If you break down the word, it sounds like "Sara-bell," or at least close enough for our purpose. Maybe you know someone named Sara (otherwise, this particular image probably will not work very well). Picture Sara in your mind. Now, add the bells. You do not want to add them to the picture in a predictable, ordinary way, such as visualizing Sara ringing a doorbell.

Do something outrageous if you want to remember the image; the more outrageous, the better. Picture Sara trying to carry a huge Liberty Bell in each hand. Each bell must weigh at least 400 pounds, so be sure to visualize Sara struggling with the weight. Once you have a visual image of "Sara-bell" (or *cerebellum*), you can link it to the other information: the cerebellum controls bodily balance and coordination. Picture Sara trying to walk with these bells on a balance beam or a tightrope. That is your cue for balance and coordination.

This process of using images may seem like a lot of work to remember one piece of information. Although imaging takes effort and creative thinking, it is faster and more effective than staring at the information until you remember it. When you "do something" with the material, you are much more likely to remember it. What is the name of that part of the brain we just talked about, and what is its function? You will still remember Sara and her bell-balancing act a month from now.

It is helpful to remember two things about using visual images to improve memory. First, imaging takes practice to get good at it, and it takes time to come up with memorable images. As you continue using the strategy over time, however, you will be able to devise images more quickly.

Second, the cornier, the more outrageous the image, the more memorable it will be. Striking images are simply easier to remember than ordinary ones. It may seem silly to sit there picturing cows in high heels (or whatever), but it works. The bottom line is that you want to remember the material in as little time as possible, and imagery is an effective way of accomplishing that goal. Select several terms from the psychology chapter you are currently reading that lend themselves well to imagery. Create an outrageous image for each term.

Vocabulary Cards

Vocabulary cards look like flash cards, but there is a slight difference that ends up making a big difference in how well you can learn vocabulary. These cards use imagery to help you remember definitions. Here's how you make a vocabulary card. First, take an index card and on the front, write the word that you think is important to know. In the upper right-hand corner, write a key term that helps you see the relationship between the concept and the "big picture." In the upper left-hand corner, put the page number on which the word and its definition are found in the textbook. If applicable, write the name of a person associated with the term in one of the bottom corners. (It really does not matter what information you put in which corner.) On the back of the card, write the term's definition. Then, come up with an image that helps you remember the definition of the concept. Draw the image on both the front and back of the card, so that you will always pair the image with the word and with the definition of the word.

For example, let's say you are reading about Freud, and you think that his "defense mechanisms" are good concepts to learn (follow along in Figure 5.1 on page 94). One of the defense mechanisms is **sublimation.** Sublimation occurs when we take a socially undesirable impulse and find an acceptable way to express it. People who like to be violent toward other people have socially undesirable impulses. But if they rechannel that desire into becoming world-class boxers, they have sublimated their violent impulses into a socially acceptable form. Write the term *sublimation* on the front of the index card and the page number on which the definition occurs in the textbook in the upper left-hand corner. Because it is from the "Motivation" chapter (it might be in the "Personality" chapter in your text), you write *Motivation* in the upper right-hand corner. You write *Freud,* the person associated with the concept, in another corner. Then you write the definition on the back. Now, the real work begins: thinking of an effective image. How about this? Picture a criminal standing in front of a mirror, a knife in one hand and a gun in the other. His reflection shows the same guy standing in the same position, but now he is wearing boxing trunks. His weapons are now boxing gloves. Somehow, you have to tie the term *sublimation* in to this image. Let's put a submarine in the criminal's mouth, and a lime in the boxer's mouth—"sub" and "lime" for "sub-lim-ation." If this image is too elaborate for you to draw, just draw the sub, and it should do the trick. Remember to put the image on both the front and back of the card.

When you use the cards to study, first look at the term and see if you can remember the definition. If not, look at the key term—is your memory jogged yet? How about the name of the person associated with the term—does that help? Now, turn to the image. The image should do the trick. If it does not, as a last resort, check the definition on the back. If you are confused by the definition you wrote, turn to the page where the word and its definition can be found, and read the section again to clarify how the term relates to the "big picture" we keep talking about.

Some chapters have more new terms in them than others, and you may end up with a big pile of cards. Do not panic at the number of cards to be learned. You have organized the information meaningfully, and thus you will be able to learn it more quickly and effectively than if you had simply tried to memorize.

As you go through the cards and overlearn the information, sort the cards into two piles: the terms you know really well and the ones you still need to learn. Take the cards with you to class so that you can study

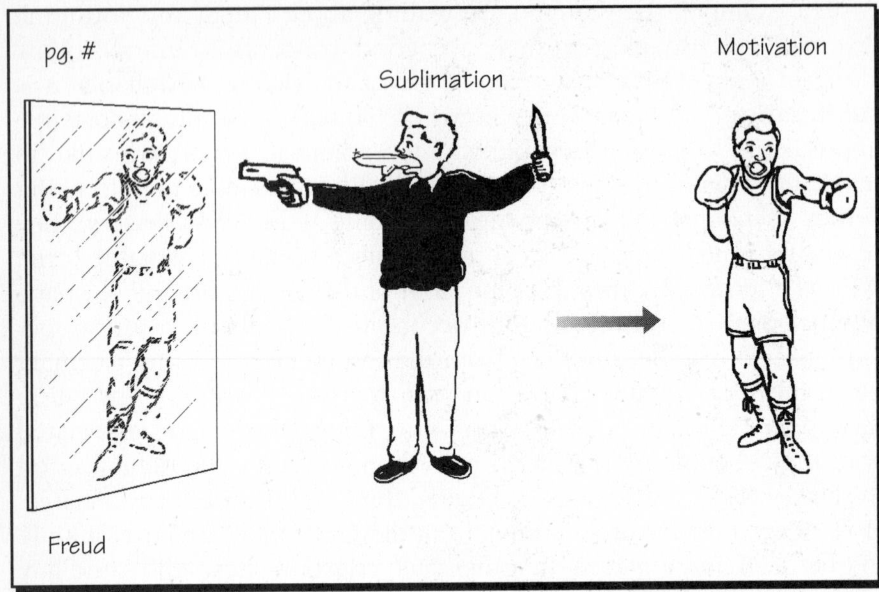

(front)

(back)

Figure 5.1 A sample vocabulary card for the word *sublimation*

them during any "dead time" you have, such as riding on the bus or waiting before a class starts.

A few reminders about imagery: it takes practice to get good at it, it takes time to come up with memorable images, and the more outrageous the image, the better. Select the important words to know in the psychology chapter you are currently reading, and create a vocabulary card for each one. Use the images you created in the previous exercise on the cards.

Mapping

Mapping is a strategy that uses a visual display to show relationships among concepts. Maps can take a lot of forms. They may look like pyramids, webs, circles, trees, graphs, or anything else you want. The important thing is that the display shows the relationships among the terms. Here are a few examples of what maps can do for you.

In the compare/contrast map on the theories of emotion (Table 5.2), you have the basic information you need on each theory and an example to help you remember the differences. At the bottom of the map, you could write a couple of sentences that describe similarities and differences between the theories. This map would help you learn the information for multiple choice, true/false, or short answer questions, but it would be especially helpful for preparing for an essay question asking you to compare and contrast the theories.

In the hierarchical map on Piaget's ideas about mental functioning (see Figure 5.2 on page 97), notice that the structure of the map can help you remember the facts. If you can learn not only the information but what it looks like on the map, with larger ideas branching off into smaller ones, your memory for the information is likely to be better.

The map of **Piaget's** four stages of cognitive development is set up as a list so that you remember that children move through each stage progressively, one after the other. Also notice that there are several terms, such as **object permanence, egocentric, operations,** and **conservation,** that are not defined in the map. If you wish, you can write a definition for each term, but it may be more effective if you have a vocabulary card for each. Although this may seem like doubling your workload, you are actually providing yourself with a few different ways to learn the same information. Thus, if your memory for what was on the map escapes you during the test, you may still have the memory of what you had on your vocabulary cards or in your annotations.

TABLE 5.2 COMPARE/CONTRAST MAP

THEORIES OF EMOTION			
Theory name	James-Lange	Cannon-Bard	Schachter-Singer
Also known as:	Body reaction theory	Central neural theory	Cognitive-arousal theory; two-factor theory
Theory's description of how emotions work	1. You perceive an event. 2. Your body reacts. 3. You interpret the reaction as a specific emotion.	1. You perceive an event. 2. Your thalamus is activated. 3. Your body reacts and you interpret the reaction simultaneously.	1. You perceive an event. 2. Your body reacts and you interpret the emotion. 3. You experience the emotion.
Example	1. Someone insults you. 2. You hit him. 3. You feel angry.	1. Someone insults you. 2. The thalamus is activated. 3. You feel angry and hit him at the same time.	1. Someone insults you. 2. Your heart starts to pound, and you label the feeling as anger. 3. You hit him.

The webs of different views of traits (Figure 5.3 on page 98) are very simple and serve to remind us of which psychologists or views identified which traits, and the traits of interest. These webs help you to discuss and recall the names of the traits associated with each view and the similarities and differences among the views. Again, you could supplement the webs with a questioning guide.

These are just a few examples of styles and shapes that maps can take. The more creative and imaginative you are, the easier the information will be to remember. It is important to be logical when figuring out what to map and how to map a set of concepts. For example, you would not use a compare/contrast map for concepts where noting similarities and differences is not helpful. In psychology, you often need to compare and contrast theories, such as in the example where we compared and contrasted the different theories of emotion. But it would not make sense to compare and contrast Piaget's stages of cognitive development—you just want to remember them in the right order.

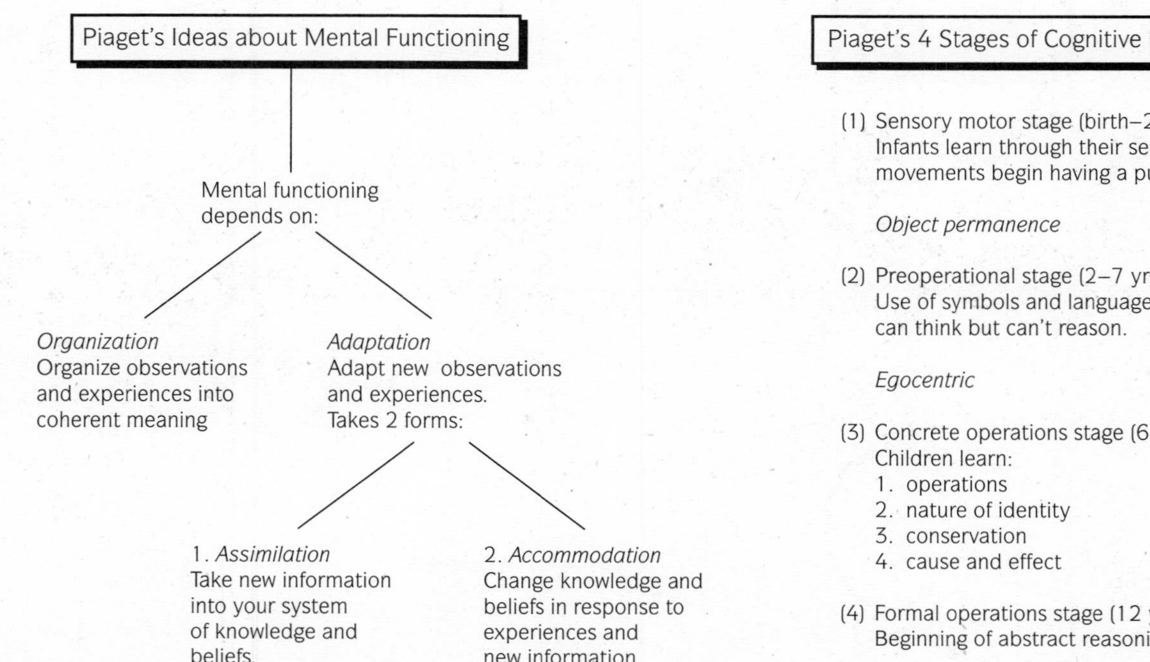

Figure 5.2 A hierarchical map and list for Piaget's Theory of Cognitive Development

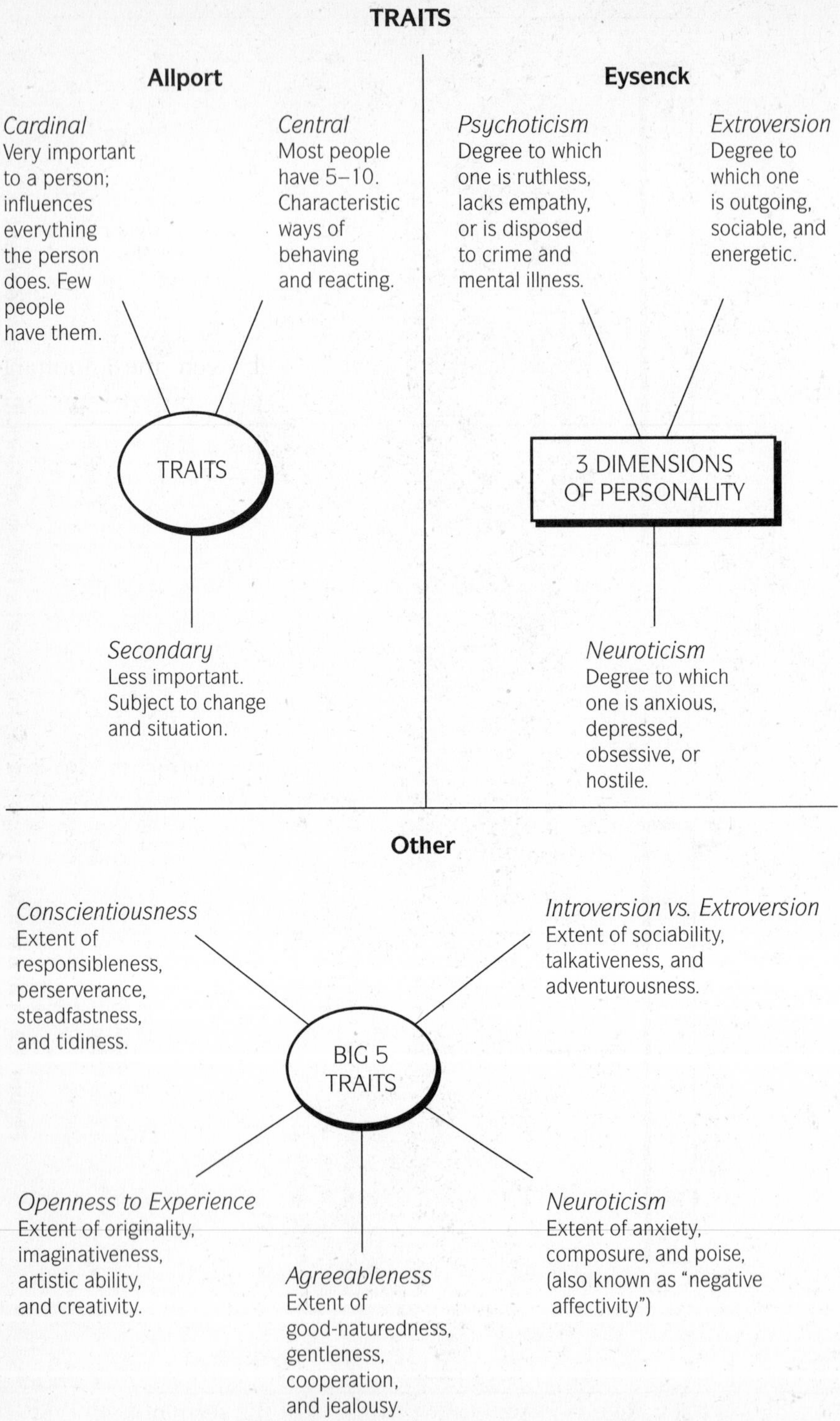

TRAITS
Allport
Cardinal
Very important to a person; influences everything the person does. Few people have them.
Central
Most people have 5–10. Characteristic ways of behaving and reacting.
TRAITS
Secondary
Less important. Subject to change and situation.
Eysenck
Psychoticism
Degree to which one is ruthless, lacks empathy, or is disposed to crime and mental illness.
Extroversion
Degree to which one is outgoing, sociable, and energetic.
3 DIMENSIONS OF PERSONALITY
Neuroticism
Degree to which one is anxious, depressed, obsessive, or hostile.
Other
Conscientiousness
Extent of responsibleness, perserverance, steadfastness, and tidiness.
Introversion vs. Extroversion
Extent of sociability, talkativeness, and adventurousness.
BIG 5 TRAITS
Openness to Experience
Extent of originality, imaginativeness, artistic ability, and creativity.
Agreeableness
Extent of good-naturedness, gentleness, cooperation, and jealousy.
Neuroticism
Extent of anxiety, composure, and poise, (also known as “negative affectivity”)

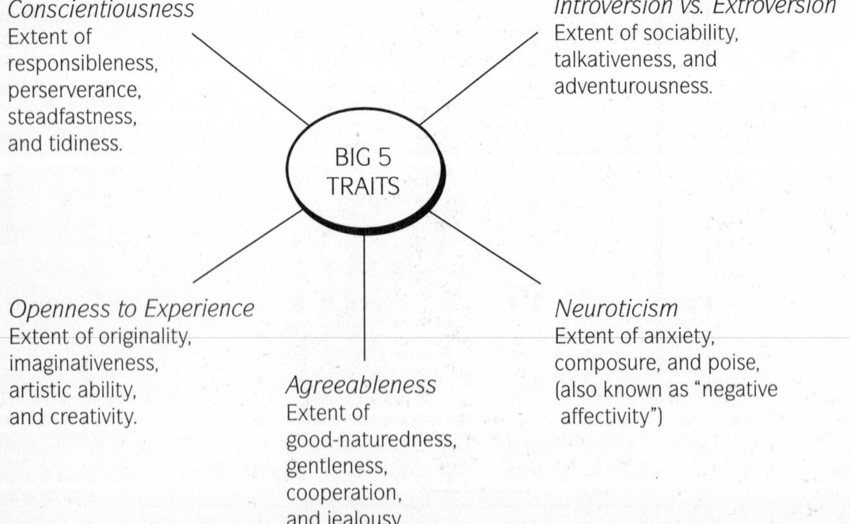

Figure 5.3 Sample webs for three different trait theories

However, if your textbook described someone else's theory of cognitive development in addition to Piaget's, you would probably want to compare and contrast the two theories.

Notice that all the maps have some things in common. First, they concentrate on the most central, important concepts. Second, they require that you reduce the amount of information to be learned. For example, the discussion about Piaget's theory of child cognitive development takes up four or five pages in the textbook we used. We reduced it to one page, just by focusing on what we thought were the important points. Third, the maps show how several concepts relate to one another, which will help you remember the material.

It requires practice to get good at making maps, but the strategy is effective. When you start to make a map, think about the passage's key idea, the subcategories, and the supporting details and examples. Do not try to put too much information in a map; make more maps rather than try to get all the important ideas on one page. At the other extreme, if you only have a few words on a map, the idea is probably not as important as you first thought. A vocabulary card might be a more appropriate strategy to use.

Examine the chapter you are currently reading in your psychology textbook. What sections or complex concepts lend themselves well to mapping? Experiment with different kinds of maps in order to find the clearest, best way for you to learn the information via mapping.

LEARN THE LINGO

Like most fields, psychology has its share of confusing, technical language. It is crucial to learn these words for two reasons. First, it is impossible to understand psychology if you do not speak the language of psychology. It is like going to Japan and trying to understand Japanese culture without being able to speak Japanese.

The second reason that it is crucial to learn psychological terms is that most psychology instructors devote many test questions to testing students' understanding of psychological terminology. You may have a terrific grasp of the underlying ideas in psychology, but if this understanding is not backed up with a knowledge of the terminology that is used to talk about these ideas, you will be in trouble at test time.

APPLICATION EXERCISES

1. What are the main concepts introduced in the psychology chapter you are currently reading for class?

   ____

   ____

   ____

   How much or how little do you already know about them? How do they relate to each other?

   ____

   ____

2. Examine the terms you must know for your next psychology test. Will structural analysis help you learn their meanings?

   ____

3. Use the vocabulary study strategies discussed in this chapter in studying the terminology for your next psychology test. Experiment with all of them, where appropriate.

TERMS TO KNOW

cerebellum
circadian rhythm
concepts
continuous reinforcement
conservation
deviance
ego
egocentric
intermittent reinforcement
memory
narcissism
negative reinforcement
object permanence
operations
pheromone
Piaget
positive reinforcement
projection
sublimation
voyeur

CHAPTER 6

MAXIMIZING YOUR MEMORY

GETTING FOCUSED

- *How does memory work?*
- *What memory tricks (mnemonics) can you use?*
- *How can you improve your memory?*

▪

PERSONAL LEARNING QUESTIONS

What do you already know about memory? Do you have a "good memory"? What strategies or tricks do you use to remember things?

▪

Some people can look at a page full of numbers for a few seconds and then repeat those numbers back, in order, without making a mistake. Some have even been able to repeat the numbers back fifteen years later! This skill is commonly known as possessing a photographic memory, also known as using **eidetic imagery.** Most people, however, have to work hard and be creative to remember material. Maximizing your memory can save you a lot of time and anguish over the course of your college career.

This chapter serves two purposes. First, memory is a topic you will almost certainly learn about in introductory psychology, so this will serve as a good introduction to the topic. Perhaps more importantly, however, learning how memory works will help you in studying, test preparation, and test taking. Therefore, we believe that it is worth repeating some of the information you will read about in the memory chapter in your psychology textbook because this material will help you become a more successful learner. In addition, we have included many examples of how to use the suggested memory improvement strategies.

MEMORY IS NOT THE SAME AS INTELLIGENCE

Before we get into the details, it is important to know that memory is not the same as intelligence. You cannot do much to change how intelligent you are. You can certainly improve your grades and become a better learner, but your intelligence, as measured by an IQ test, will not waver very much over your lifetime. Your memory, on the other hand, is something that is very much within your control. You can improve it dramatically if you want to put time and effort into it.

Jerry Lucas, a former professional basketball player and current coach, was able to memorize the entire Manhattan phone book. He memorized every name, every address, every phone number. He does not have a photographic memory—he did it with the same kind of memory that most of us have. Granted, Mr. Lucas devoted a great deal of time learning and practicing strategies that give him such a remarkable memory.

The point is that people can and do improve their memory drastically. To a great extent, memory is a skill that you develop, rather than a gift with which you are born. A good memory is a valuable tool for a student. Because students spend a great deal of time trying to remember information, it is a good idea for students to take the time to learn how to improve memory.

Before we talk about some specific techniques that you can use to improve memory, let's take a look at how memory works. The techniques for improving memory will make more sense if you understand how your memory operates.

HOW MEMORY WORKS

Psychologists disagree on exactly how memory works, but they commonly talk as if there were an actual physical place where you put information until you need to remember it. Actually, they talk about two distinct "places" in which you hold information: short-term memory and long-term memory.

Short-term Memory

Short-term memory can be thought of as a work space. The facts you hold here are those you need right now, such as a phone number you are about to call or a list of a few items you are going to buy at the grocery store. Information does not stay very long in short-term memory—the range is five to thirty seconds. If you want to keep something in short-term memory for longer than five to thirty seconds, you have to keep renewing it by **rehearsal.** Rehearsal means repeating it over and over, such as saying a phone number over and over to remember it if you do not have a pen to write it down. It is essential to rehearse information in short-term memory in order to eventually store it.

Short-term memory does not have much space. It can hold about seven pieces of information, give or take about two, at one time. This number, seven plus or minus two, is often called the **magic number.** (This fact is likely to show up as a test question.) These seven pieces of information can be seven numbers, seven grocery items, seven names, or whatever. If you are holding something in short-term memory and you forget it, it is most likely gone forever. There is no hidden space in short-term memory.

Because short-term memory can neither hold much information nor hold it for very long, and the information is gone for good once you lose it, it is not a good place to store important information. It is fine for grocery items but not recommended for information you need to know for a test. The place you want to put test information is in long-term memory.

Test the limits of your short-term memory. Have someone list aloud a string of five numbers or words. Repeat them back immediately. Can you remember them in order? Now try six numbers or words, then seven. What are the limits of your short-term memory?

Long-term Memory

Long-term memory is the storehouse for information that is to be kept for a long time. It is a big storehouse. In fact, it seems to have a limitless capacity. We can continue putting in more and more information, and long-term memory never seems to get full. Also, many psychologists believe that once information is in long-term memory, it is there for good. You never really forget anything that goes into your long-term memory.

So, why can't you remember who sat next to you in first grade? Here is the problem: because there is so much information in long-term memory, some of it can get "lost." The piece you are looking for is in there, but you just cannot find it. In psychological terms, this is called having problems with **retrieval.**

Think of your long-term memory as a huge library. If everything were filed away perfectly, it would always be easy to find things. But imagine that some of the librarians in this library have gotten a little careless. They may not always put things away in exactly the right place, later making the information hard to find in this huge library... but the information is there somewhere.

A library is a good analogy for long-term memory because memories are usually filed away according to subject matter. Try to think of the name of your second-grade teacher. Notice that when you come up with the name, you also remember a few related memories. They are not memories of an eighth-grade dance or what you ate for dinner last Thanksgiving. They are memories from second grade, because second-grade memories are filed together. Memories can also be cross-referenced, that is, filed in more than one place. You may also have the name of your second-grade teacher filed in a list of all of your grade-school teachers.

We do not necessarily have memories of everything that has ever happened to us stored in long-term memory. Some of our experiences are turned into memories, or **encoded,** and some are not. Let's take a look at some of the reasons a piece of information might make it into long-term memory.

How Information Gets in Long-term Memory

Information can end up in long-term memory for a number of different reasons. Very striking or remarkable things or events go into long-term memory without any real effort on your part. For example, where were you when you found out that the space shuttle *Challenger* had exploded? You probably remember the moment clearly, and you can probably remember a lot of details about who you were with and what was said at the time. When something truly "memorable" happens, we remember it. Relying on this process is not very helpful for studying, though, since we rarely come across information in a textbook that is as startling or emotionally moving as an assassination or natural disaster.

Another way information gets into long-term memory is by chance. Some information just happens to stick in our memory. We remember many everyday, boring things from our past. You may remember buying a tube of toothpaste five years ago, or playing in your room with a particular toy when you were a child. Some of the material you need to remember for a test will just enter and remain in your memory by chance. Hoping that all the information you need for a test will be in your memory by chance, however, is not a good bet.

A third way that information gets into long-term memory is through **repetition.** We usually learn phone numbers through repetition. As we look up a phone number and dial it again and again, eventually we commit it to memory. This method of studying is used by many students. They sit with their notes in front of them, reading over the material again and again. This is a better strategy than hoping the material ends up in long-term memory by chance, or hoping for a natural disaster while you are looking at the information. But it takes a long time to memorize this way, and it is unreliable. Often, you have trouble retrieving the information at test time. More importantly, you may have simply memorized material without thinking critically about it—without having truly learned it.

Some memory strategies focus on simply remembering information at a rather shallow level; others deal more with learning information at deeper levels. When you study, you will need both kinds of strategies. Here we will present a few memory tricks that will help you remember information, although your actual learning of it may be at a rather shallow level. In Chapters 7 and 8, we will present strategies that help you learn information even more meaningfully.

THE THREE MAIN WAYS INFORMATION GETS INTO LONG-TERM MEMORY

1. By something striking or memorable happening.
2. By chance.
3. By repetition.

USING MEMORY TRICKS

Memory tricks are called **mnemonics.** The most popular and useful mnemonics involve using imagery, method of loci, and acronyms.

Using Imagery

This strategy should be familiar from Chapter 5. Remember "Sara-bell" for *cerebellum?* When you try to come up with an image to remember a word, keep in mind that the image needs to reflect the meaning of the word, such as Sara struggling with two huge bells to reflect the cerebellum's role in balance and coordination.

Using Imagery to Remember Phobias Let's go through another example using **imagery** as a memory tool, because this is a great strategy for remembering psychological concepts. In all likelihood, you will learn about the different types of phobias from which people can suffer. The concept of a phobia is straightforward enough: a phobia is an irrational fear of some thing or event. People with phobias have irrational fears of such things as closed-in spaces, heights, snakes, cats, and math. The difficult part about learning about phobias is that each phobia has a particular name and the names are not easily remembered. Let's take five common phobias and work with them:

Acrophobia:	Fear of heights
Claustrophobia:	Fear of cramped or closed-in places
Ophidiophobia:	Fear of snakes
Hematophobia:	Fear of blood
Agoraphobia:	Fear of open spaces and unfamiliar places

Now, let's create a visual image to link each phobia to its meaning. First of all, forget about remembering the *phobia* ending of each term. We're sure you'll remember that each of these words consists of a prefix followed by the word *phobia* so just focus on learning the prefixes.

Acro is similar to *acrobat.* Picture an acrobat on the trapeze. The problem, however, is that this acrobat has acrophobia, so the trapeze is only 6 inches off the ground.

The next phobia is claustrophobia. "Claustro-" sounds a little like "closet," which is a closed-in space that might give a claustrophobic trouble. Picture a claustrophobic person locked in a closet, screaming to get out.

Ophidiophobia is a fear of snakes. It is a little tougher to come up with an image for this phobia. Perhaps you could picture a snake biting its own tail so that it forms a big "O." Remembering that the first letter of the word is *O* should prompt you to recall *ophidio-*.

"Hemato-" sounds something like "he-man." Picture a big, muscular "he-man" crying and carrying on because he has a small paper cut with one drop of blood welling up in it. He has "heman-ophobia," better known as hematophobia.

Agoraphobia is one of the most difficult phobias to live with. It is not as difficult to avoid something like snakes or closed-in places as it is to avoid open spaces and unfamiliar places. As soon as you step outside your door, you are in an open space. Many agoraphobics stay in their houses for years at a time. "Agora-" sounds similar to the beginning of "agriculture." Of course, agriculture involves planting fields of crops in wide open spaces, which is not the place to be if you suffer from agoraphobia. Visualize a wide open field and think of it as "agoraculture" rather than "agriculture."

Look for terminology in the psychology chapter you are currently reading that lends itself well to imagery. Devise an effective image for each term.

Using Your House as a Memory Tool: Method of Loci

Your house, or any place you know very well, can help you remember things. This strategy is called **method of loci** (location). Imagine that you have a list of things that you have to remember in a particular order. One topic you are likely to encounter in psychology class that fits this description is **Maslow's "hierarchy of needs."**[1] According to the hierarchy of needs, people are rarely motivated to pursue loftier needs or goals if they have not yet satisfied more basic needs. The order of these needs is:

1. Physiological needs: Food, water, oxygen
2. Safety needs: A safe home, security, freedom from fear
3. Belongingness and love needs: The need for friends and love
4. Esteem needs: Self-esteem, respect, approval from others
5. Cognitive needs: The need for knowledge, understanding
6. Aesthetic needs: Beauty, art
7. Self-actualization: The need to reach your highest potential
8. Enlightenment: Spiritual fulfillment

The theory states that you will not be interested in a need on a higher level (higher number) if you are still struggling with a need on a lower level (lower number). For example, you will not care about having beautiful art on the wall (aesthetic need) if you have no friends or loved ones (belongingness and love needs).

---

[1]A. H. Maslow, *Motivation and Personailty,* 2nd ed. (1954; rpt., New York: HarperCollins, 1970).

It is clearly important to remember these needs in order because the order is the key to the whole theory. One way to remember the order is to take a mental walking tour of your house and put one of the needs in each of the rooms. Try to visualize the tour happening in your own house or apartment.

Walking Through Maslow's Hierarchy Start by stepping through the front door into the hall. The hall is filled with bread, knee deep. You will never go hungry in here (physiological needs). Next is the living room. A large orange sign flashes, "Construction ahead—Safety first!" Cushions cover the floor in case someone trips. Obviously, safety is a primary concern in the living room (safety needs). Go into the kitchen and over to the stove to see what is cooking on one of the burners. You lift the lid on a pot and see a human heart cooking (belongingness and love needs—get it?—heart). Out on the back porch, you find huge mail bags full of fan mail, all addressed to you. Your self-esteem rises (esteem needs).

Back inside, you head up the stairs. You have a lot of trouble getting up the stairs because there are brains all over them (cognitive needs). You slip and slide, and finally make it to the top. In the bedroom, beautiful flowers are everywhere, sticking out of drawers, lying in piles on the floor, and strewn all over the bed. Famous works of art hang on the walls, like the Mona Lisa and Whistler's Mother (aesthetic needs). In the bathroom are several people who have reached their full potential. Abe Lincoln is in the shower, Beethoven is washing his hands, and Gandhi is shaving his head. These are **self-actualized** people in the bathroom. As you come to the final room, the den, you open the door, and you are blinded. You shield your eyes; you cannot even go in. The room is enlightened.

We have made a few of these images rather vivid. We chose these images because outrageous, funny, or disgusting images are more easily remembered than boring ones.

You can use the "house method" (method of loci) for just about any list, even if you do not care about the order of the items. It works well for remembering grocery lists. Now, mentally walk through the house again. Through the hall, living room, kitchen, back porch, stairs, bedroom, bathroom, and den. If you think you have gotten the hierarchy of needs down, try this question:

A person is unlikely to strive to attain ______ if he or she has not yet attained ______

a. self-esteem; an appreciation of beauty
b. enough to eat; a mate
c. self-actualization; a safe place to live
d. knowledge; enlightenment

The correct answer is c. A person is unlikely to want something higher in the hierarchy of needs (self-actualization) if he or she has a lower need that is unfulfilled (a safe place to live).

▪

PERSONAL LEARNING QUESTIONS

List Maslow's hierarchy using the method of loci. Don't look back to check yourself until you are done.

▪

Walking Through Piaget's Stages of Cognitive Development The method of loci can be used with other locations besides your house. Do you like to shop? If so, you can use the stores in a mall or the stores on a main street in your town. You can also create a fictitious shopping area to suit your needs. To demonstrate this, we will go through Piaget's four stages of cognitive development, which you are sure to learn in introductory psychology.[2] (Recall that you already saw a map of Piaget's four stages in Chapter 5.) To review, Piaget's four stages of cognitive development describe changes in how we think as we grow from infancy to adulthood. In order, the stages and their central features are:

1. Sensory motor stage: You begin to explore your environment.
2. Preoperational stage: You are egocentric and able to use symbols.
3. Concrete operations: You understand the laws of conservation.
4. Formal operations: You are capable of abstract thinking.

In order to remember these stages using the method of loci, we will walk down a fictional street and look in on four businesses: a car dealership, a clothing store, a bakery, and a bridal shop.

---

[2] J. Piaget, *The Child's Conception of the World.* (Paterson, NJ: Littlefield, Adams, 1960.) (First published in English in 1929.)

As you start your walking tour, the car dealer shows you a sports car with an engine that has just recently been developed. It is called a sensory motor (**sensory motor stage**). The dealer lifts the hood, and you see that the engine is made up of all sorts of noses, eyes, ears, and tongues (sense organs). You hop in the car for a test drive, and explore your environment.

Then, you head to your favorite clothing store. Surprisingly, all of the usual clothing is gone. They are only selling surgical garb—surgical gowns, gloves, and masks. This store is the place to go if you are getting ready to perform an operation (**preoperational stage**). You are distracted by two children who are fighting over a surgical gown. The gown is embroidered with all sorts of symbols: question marks, hearts, and smiley faces. The children are yelling, "Mine! Mine!" as they fight over the gown. Both children are clearly egocentric because they are not willing to share: they are only thinking of themselves.

As you continue down the street, cakes and pies in the bakery window catch your eye, and you go in. There are no nice smells in this bakery, however; in fact, the smell of concrete is in the air. Upon closer examination, you find that all of the baked goods in this bakery are made out of concrete! You spy some people dressed in surgical garb (which they probably got from the preoperational clothing store). They are performing an operation, using a slice of concrete pie as a scalpel (a **concrete operation**). In another area of the bakery, a baker is pouring concrete from a tall, thin vat into a squat, wide vat. She asks another baker if there is as much concrete in the wide vat as there had been in the tall vat. The other baker answers "Yes," demonstrating his ability in making judgments of **conservation.**

The final store you visit is a bridal shop. You peek in the window and find more people performing operations. These surgeons are dressed in evening gowns and tuxedos—these are **formal operations.** All of the surgeons, both men and women, look like philosophers. They have long, gray beards and thoughtful expressions on their faces. They are clearly engrossed in abstract thinking as they operate.

▪

Personal Learning Questions

List Piaget's four stages of cognitive development using the method of loci. Don't look back to check yourself until you are done.

▪

Using Acronyms

Still another method of remembering lists is through the use of **acronyms** and other similar devices. If you took music class in grade school, you might remember the sentence Every Good Boy Does Fine that is often used to help people remember the lines on a musical staff (EGBDF). If you do remember this device, think about it: what are the chances that you would remember EGBDF from music class seven or eight years ago if you did not use the sentence to remember it? Doing something with the material you want to remember helps you retain that material.

FLOP Here is an example of using an acronym to remember something from psychology. Let's try another brain example, because the unfamiliar words given to different parts of the brain are usually difficult to remember. The four lobes of the brain are: frontal, lateral, occipital, and parietal. (In some textbooks, the lateral lobe is called the temporal lobe.) When you put them in this order, notice that the first letters spell out FLOP. Often, the first letter of a word is enough to jar the entire word out of your memory. Just remember that if you drop the lobes of a brain on a cold stone floor, the sound they make is "flop."

Drug Classifications Another similar technique that comes in handy involves taking each word from the list you are trying to remember and replacing it with another word that begins with the same letter. Choose words that make a sentence that is easy for you to remember. A couple of examples of this technique will make this a bit clearer.

Your introductory psychology class will likely cover drug use, and if it does, you will be required to know the classification of each drug that is covered. Drugs are classified based on the effect they have on people. The classification of the major drugs is as follows:

Stimulants: amphetamines, nicotine, caffeine, cocaine
Depressants: barbiturates, opium, alcohol
Hallucinogens: marijuana, LSD

Using the first letter from each of these words, we came up with these sentences:

Stimulants Are Not Causing Calmness
Depressants Bring On Apathy
Hallucinogens Make Little Sheep Dance

These sentences should be easy to remember because the sentences are related to the drug classifications. Stimulants make people very alert and energetic, so they definitely do not contribute to calmness. Depressants are "downers"; they make people very calm and relaxed, which could cause them to feel apathetic. Hallucinogens can cause people to hallucinate, so they may see strange things like "little sheep dancing." Notice on the hallucinogen example we "cheated" a bit. Because it would be difficult to make up a sentence using only the letters *h, m,* and *l,* we used all of the letters in *LSD.* In this case, however, cheating is permitted because there are no hard and fast rules in devising memory aids—you use whatever works. To review, what are the names of the lobes of the brain? What are the drug classifications? Don't look back to check yourself until you have recalled as much as possible.

OTHER TIPS TO IMPROVE MEMORY

Practice, Practice, Practice

We said earlier that long-term memory is like a huge library. It is also like a funnel. Although long-term memory is limitless, there is a limit to how much information you can put in at once. Memorizing works best if you do it like you would pour something through a funnel. You pour a little, then wait, then pour some more. If you pour liquid through a funnel all at once, most of it spills onto the floor.

Although we will deal with time management, studying, and test preparation in later chapters, here is an inportant tip to think about now. If you plan on studying for a particular test for five hours, you will get much more out of the five hours if you spread it out into ten half-hour sessions over a couple of days. If you study for five straight hours the night before the exam, much of what you try to memorize will just "spill out." You have to give things a chance to sink in. This is called "distributed versus massed practice." **Distributed practice** is spreading out study time, while **massed practice** is "cramming." Time management is the key factor in making distributed practice work.

Watch the Middle: The Serial Position Effect

Remember Maslow and his hierarchy of needs? If not, walk through the house we set up earlier and retrieve that memory. What need was in the bathroom? The self-actualized individuals (Lincoln, Gandhi, and Beethoven) were in the bathroom, so self-actualization was the need associated with the bathroom. Maslow developed a list of characteristics that most self-actualized people share, and we are going to make use of that list to demonstrate this memory tip. Read through this list of characteristics one by one and try to remember each characteristic. Do not go back over them more than once, just read the list from first characteristic to last. Have a piece of paper and a pen ready.

Characteristics of Self-actualized Individuals

1. They are highly creative.

2. They focus on solving problems, not on furthering their own self-interest.

3. They are spontaneous.

4. They have a good sense of humor, but not at the expense of other people.

5 They have a great need for privacy.

6. They accept themselves and others as they are.

7. They are realistic, and they want the truth whether it is good or bad.

8. They have a childlike appreciation of life.

9. They often have mystical or spiritual experiences.

10. They feel a part of humankind as a whole, rather than feeling loyal to any one nation.

11. They tend to have only a few friends, but they are very close to those friends.

Look away from the list and write down as many of the characteristics as you can. When you finish, put a check next to each of the characteristics that you correctly recalled. Do you see any pattern to the characteristics you recalled and those you did not? Most people will tend to forget the information in the middle more than the information at the beginning or the end.

Whenever you have to learn something that has a beginning, a middle, and an end, remember that you are very likely to recall the beginning and the end better than the middle. This phenomenon is called the **serial position effect**[3] or sometimes the **primacy/recency effect.** If you study a set of lecture notes in the same order every time, you will know the notes on the beginning and end pages better than the notes on middle pages. Why? Psychologists think it is because the information at the end is still in your short-term memory, the information at the beginning has been rehearsed and is in your long-term memory, and thus the information in the middle is easily forgotten.

You can counter this problem in two ways. If there is no reason to keep material in a certain order, rotate it so that it is in the middle only some of the time. If it is important that the information stay in a particular order (like the hierarchy of needs), give the middle additional time, and use an effective mnemonic like imagery or method of loci.

It's in There; Now How Do I Get it Out?

Let's assume you have everything you need to know safely tucked away in long-term memory. Now you want to make sure you can get it

[3]M. Glanzer and A. R. Cunitz, "Two Storage Mechanisms in Free Recall," *Journal of Verbal Learning and Verbal Behavior,* 5, 1966, 351—360.

out again during a test or for your own needs. The concept of **state-dependent learning** is important here. If you study at your desk in your dorm room, the easiest place to recall the information is at your desk in your dorm room. Generally, you are more likely to remember something if you are in a situation and frame of mind similar to when you first committed the information to memory. If you are in your pajamas eating a peanut butter and jelly sandwich when you study, these same conditions can help trigger recall of that information later. Why?

Evidently, when we file information in long-term memory, it is not only filed by topic, such as "parts of the brain"; it is also filed under "things I memorized while in my pajamas," or "things I memorized when I was depressed." Although you cannot take a test in your pajamas while eating peanut butter, you can mentally recreate the environment in which you studied. This method actually works just as well as being there.

Also remember that you most likely studied when you were in a calm frame of mind. Therefore, your recall will be best if you are calm and relaxed during the test.

It's on the Tip of My Tongue

Ever try to remember a word or phrase, and you know you know it, but you cannot seem to get it out? You may know how many syllables the word has or the letter the word begins with, but you cannot recall the word itself. This is called the tip-of-the-tongue state or phenomenon.[4] Let's say you were given the following test question:

> *When other people are present, we perform simple tasks faster and difficult tasks more slowly than when other people are not present. This phenomenon is called ________.*

You have learned the correct term, and you know it is two words, and you know that the second word is four or five syllables long and has the sound "sill" in it. You are suffering from **tip-of-the-tongue phenomenon,** which can be especially frustrating if you are in the middle of a test. There is nothing like getting a test item wrong when you know the answer is in your memory somewhere.

---

[4]R. Brown and D. McNeill, "The 'Tip of the Tongue' Phenomenon," *Journal of Verbal Learning and Verbal Behavior,* 5, 1966, 325–337.

You can try two things when you have a case of "tip of the tongue." First, try mentally repeating everything you know about the word or phrase you are trying to remember. How many syllables does the word have? What is the first letter? What are some of the other letters in the word? What does it sound like? Often, the word will spring to mind.

If the first strategy does not work, send a work order down to whomever or whatever is in charge of finding information in your memory, and go on to the next question. No, you did not misread that last sentence. Did you ever notice how information that you are trying to remember often "pops" into your mind later on, when you are not even thinking about it? Obviously, some other part of your mind is still working on finding what you want to remember while you are preoccupied with something else. If you cannot remember a word, you cannot bully your memory into finding it. The harder you push, the further away the word often slips. Your best bet is to make a mental note that you are going to move on, but you will return later and try again. Often, the information shows up while you are working on something else. By the way, the answer to the test question is **social facilitation.**

If learning just consisted of memorizing, we could end the book right here. However, to truly learn from text and lecture and to understand how psychology relates to real life, you need to be able to process information at deeper levels than memorization provides.

APPLICATION EXERCISES

1. Explore your long-term memory. We all use our long-term memory, but we rarely examine it carefully. Logically, the better we understand how it works, the better use we can make of it. Sometime when you have free time in a quiet place, explore your long-term memory.

   Choose a time and place in your life. See how much detail you can retrieve. Try to unlock old, forgotten memories. Watch how you are doing the retrieval.

   Try long-term memory "surfing." Let your long-term memory bring up any memories it wants. How are they connected, if at all? Notice the emotions that different memories trigger.

2. Practice these memory tricks with the material in your psychology textbook: imagery, method of loci, and acronyms. Try them in other courses if appropriate.

TERMS TO KNOW

acronym
concrete operations
conservation
distributed practice
eidetic imagery
encoding
formal operations
imagery
long-term memory
magic number
Maslow's hierarchy of needs
massed practice
method of loci
mnemonics
preoperational stage
rehearsal
repetition
retrieval
self-actualization
sensory motor stage
serial position effect
primacy/recency effect
short-term memory
social facilitation
state-dependent learning
tip-of-the-tongue phenomenon

CHAPTER 7

STUDYING PSYCHOLOGY

GETTING FOCUSED

- *Do you understand the difference between reading and studying?*
- *Do you use annotations to study?*
- *How can you construct study strategy materials?*
- *What is rehearsing?*
- *How do you study with partners?*

▪

Personal Learning Questions

Jot down in the margins what you actually do when you say you "study."

▪

Here is the scenario: you have a test in psychology, covering four chapters and a couple of weeks of lecture notes. You have not read most of the material, and you have not looked at your notes since the day you took them. The test is tomorrow. You say to your friend, "I have a test tomorrow in psychology. I have to go study now."

What is wrong with this picture? You have left everything to the last minute, which is definitely not a good strategy if you want to do well in the class. In addition, you have made the classic error in thinking that reading and studying are the same thing. They are not. When you read, you are interacting with the material probably for the first time, and you are busy trying to figure out what is and is not important to know. As you annotate, you are reducing the amount of information in front of you to only what you think you need to know. When you study, you take the material that you think is important, and you do something with it. (We will get more specific about what "do something" means in just a moment.)

The two most common study techniques used by high school and college students are rereading and rewriting. These are also two of the most passive and least effective strategies you could possibly choose. They require the least amount of effort on your part, so you are working with the material in a "shallow" way. When you reread a large amount of information, you are just letting your eyes run over the material. You are not interacting with the information in any way, that is, you are not doing anything with the material. If you are confused about information when you first read it, reread it then so that you may annotate correctly. In the same way, if you merely rewrite your annotations or lecture notes in essentially the same form as when you wrote them in the first place, you are just making them neater. You are copying, which is also a form of not-studying.

So, what is studying, if not rereading and rewriting? Let us tell you a couple of other things it is not and keep you in suspense a little while longer. When we ask students what they do to study, they often say, "I look over my annotations and I go over my notes." Look over? Go over? What do you do when you "look over" and "go over"? These "strategies" are passive and indicate that you're simply staring at page after page, rereading. Rereading is not an active strategy, as we pointed out earlier.

You get the message by now. When you study, you have to do something different than stare, reread, rewrite, go over, and look over.

ACTIVE STUDYING

To be effective, studying must be done in an active mode. Studying is very much like drawing, writing, playing, thinking, or exploring. Studying is being creative. When you study, you need to interact with the material in a variety of ways. You need to get the information into your head through several different routes.

If you just memorize the fact that **Wilhelm Wundt** established the first true psychology laboratory in 1879, you only have that one route (memorization) to rely on in the test. If, by chance, you freeze, then the one route to that piece of information in your head shuts down. If, however, you studied that fact using a map, a vocabulary card, a timeline, and a question-answer strategy (which will be explained soon), you have many routes to that fact in your head. If one route shuts down, you may have two others to rely on.

You are also less likely to forget a fact if you have used strategies like mapping and cards because you have done more with the information than just memorized it. You have truly learned it. You have worked with it in different forms, elaborated on it, thought about how it related to other facts or theories in the text, drawn an image to remember it by, and asked questions about it. With the extra work, you know it well.

Think of memorizing as getting to know a person you have just met. You do not yet know this person very well, and you can only remember the most superficial things about him or her. Now, think of studying as if it were the beginning weeks of an intense romantic affair. You want to know everything you can about this person. You are fascinated by him or her, you want to spend a lot of time together, and you want to talk with each other till the wee hours. You may or may not be infatuated with psychology, but in order to do well in the course (and in any course, for that matter), you have to interact with the material and get to know it well.

MAKE USE OF YOUR HARD WORK

Remember all those annotations you wrote in your textbook? It took a lot of time to annotate—it was hard work. You picked out the information that you thought was important, wrote it in your own words as much as possible, and it has been waiting for you, stored up. Now, it is time to make use of that hard work.

Your annotations will form the basis of the information you will use in developing one or more study strategies. A *strategy,* in this case, is a plan of what you will do with the material to be learned. Mapping and charting, vocabulary cards, questioning, and timelines, for example, are strategies that will make up part of your plan for doing well on a test or paper. Notice that a strategy implies action on your part; to be good at studying, you have to be creative, conscious, deliberate, involved, and attentive.

In the rest of this chapter, we will show you the strategies that we teach our students. Try them; give them a chance. We have often heard our students say that they want to learn how to be better students, but often they do not want to try a new approach. This situation is like saying you want to be different than you are now, but you do not want to change! Most people are resistant to changing their study habits because (1) it is difficult to change, and (2) good strategies involve more work than rereading and rewriting. But more initial work is exactly what it takes to be a better student! If you get good at using these strategies, however, you will find that while you are putting in a lot of work up front, you will not be up until all hours the night before a test, wondering why you have left everything to the last minute.

Personal Learning Questions

Have you ever used any strategies besides rereading the text and rewriting your notes? If so, what did you do? Was it effective?

ACTIVE STRATEGIES FOR STUDYING PSYCHOLOGY

We will discuss four active strategies that you can use to study psychology effectively.

Questioning

You are probably familiar with this strategy, although your experience with it may have taken a different form than what we are suggesting here. Did any of your high school teachers ever provide you with a study guide to follow as you read your textbook? Did it contain a series of questions for you to answer to make sure that you focused on the most important ideas in the material? The problem with such a study guide is that someone else came up with the questions for you (so the activity was passive). Coming up with the questions yourself is a good way to learn material. The questioning strategy that we recommend involves you coming up with both the questions and the answers; in fact, making your own study guide.

Look at Table 7.1 below for an example of how to question yourself on material dealing with personality theories. This example is just the beginning of a study guide. You would include many more questions than just the few we have here. First, notice the format of the strategy: questions on the left, answers on the right. Each answer is directly across from its question for easy self-testing, instead of having each answer written underneath the question. You can cover up the answer or fold the page in half lengthwise in order to test yourself.

Next, notice that some of the questions are "what" and "who" questions. They focus on information that only requires you to learn the facts. These are the easiest questions to write. It is important to have some "why" and "how" questions also. Most instructors will not test

TABLE 7.1 QUESTIONING STRATEGY

QUESTION	ANSWER
1. What is personality?	1. Personality is a distinctive and relatively stable pattern of behavior, thoughts, motives, and emotions that characterizes an individual.
2. What are the 4 main schools of thought on personality?	2. Psychoanalysis, learning, humanism, and trait
3. Who is the founder of psychoanalysis?	3. Freud
4. How did Adler's view of personality differ from Freud's view?	4. More positive view—people want to improve themselves, not dominate others. Emphasis on people's need for others. Believed humans to be active in controlling the course of their life, not passive.

you only on the facts. They will want you to think and make connections with the material as well. Question 4 asks how Adler differed from Freud in his beliefs about personality. This information may not be neatly listed in the text, but it can be figured out by reading first about Freud's ideas and then about Adler's.

Coming up with a question like that last one demonstrates that the similarities and differences between these two psychologists are important. In fact, the text that we are using examines the differences between Freud and three other psychoanalysts: **Karen Horney, Alfred Adler,** and **Carl Jung.** The fact that several pages are spent on these differences suggests that the topic is important, and it might be wise to develop a compare/contrast map (see Table 7.2 on page 127) to examine those differences in depth for a possible essay question. Similarly, the personality chapter examines four different schools of thought on personality, and a compare/contrast map would also be appropriate.

One last word of advice on questioning and study guides: focus on the main ideas, not the picky details. Otherwise, you could end up with pages of trivia, and you do not need to waste your time focusing on unimportant material. It takes enough time to learn the important material.

▪

Personal Learning Questions

What is your first impression of this strategy? Have you ever used questioning before? Select a section of the psychology chapter you are currently reading for class that is particularly difficult for you or contains a great deal of information. Construct a study guide for that section. Remember to focus on main ideas.

▪

Timelines

Timelines are typically used in history to indicate the chronology of important events, and because chronology, sequence, and cause and effect are the major forms that history takes in textbooks. Chronology is just as important in other subject areas. In psychology, it is not necessarily crucial to remember years and dates for their own sake. It is important, however, to know when different theories were developed in order to understand how and why they evolved in the first place, or to know the sequence involved in how humans develop socially and cognitively.

Examine the timeline in Figure 7.1. Knowing the facts about social and cognitive development is necessary, and your annotations, maps, and vocabulary cards would help you remember those facts. Until you actually sketch out a timeline, however, it is difficult to remember when certain aspects of our social and cognitive behaviors develop.

You can study timelines in several ways. If the timeline shows dates and knowing dates is important, then you can cover the dates and try to remember the events, or you can cover the events and try to remember what occurred in each year. In the case of the timeline example in the figure, you can cover the ages and try to remember when different developmental behaviors occur, or cover the behaviors and try to remember them by looking at the ages. Another way to study this material is to have one vocabulary card for each aspect of social and cognitive development, yielding nine cards. Then, place them in the order you think they occur. To test your knowledge further, you could summarize the concepts in paragraph, or even essay, form.

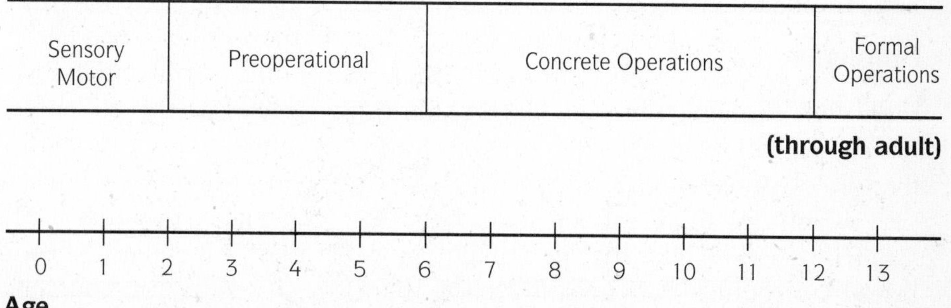

Figure 7.1 A timeline of social and cognitive development

▪

Personal Learning Questions

Have you ever used a timeline before? Keep alert for sections in your psychology text or lecture notes that would be appropriate to study using timelines.

▪

Mapping

As we mentioned in Chapter 5, mapping is a strategy that uses a visual display to show relationships among concepts. There is no one strict formula for what a map should look like. Depending on how you think about the material, maps can look like charts, webs, circles, trees, graphs, or anything else you want. The important thing is that the display shows the relationships among the concepts.

As we pointed out before, although the shapes of the maps are different, all the maps have a few things in common: (1) they concentrate on important information rather than trivial details; (2) the amount of information contained in them is greatly reduced from the amount provided in the textbook; and (3) they show the relationships among the concepts. On the next few pages, you will find a few examples to give you an idea of the forms that maps may take. (These maps are different from those in Chapter 5; we want to give you several examples.)

Compare/Contrast Map The compare/contrast map (Table 7.2) contains a lot of information, but in some ways it does not contain enough. If you were writing an essay comparing and contrasting these theories, you would not have enough information here to do a thorough job. You would need to expand the description of each theory. Also, you have to push yourself a step beyond the facts on the map to look at the important issues about the theories and how they differ from each other. To prepare more thoroughly, then, you could supplement this map with a questioning guide containing questions like these: "How does each theory explain the unconscious?" "Is human nature destructive or constructive, according to each theory?" "According to each theory, which has more influence on behavior: personality or situation?" "Which theories think that personality is stable over a lifetime?" These questions require you to study each theory and decide for yourself what the answer is.

TABLE 7.2 COMPARE/CONTRAST MAP: OVERVIEW OF PERSONALITY THEORIES

	PSYCHOANALYTIC	BEHAVIORAL	SOCIAL LEARNING	HUMANIST	TRAIT
Description of theory	Personality consists of unconscious motives and conflicts	Personality is made up of conditioned responses. Personality is nothing but behavior patterning.	Personality depends on context in which behavior is learned and the current situation in which it occurs.	Personality is determined by choice, will, and self-direction.	Personality is made up of the different traits a person possesses. Stable across time.
Main people	Freud (Horney, Adler, Jung)	Watson, Skinner	Bandura (Mischel)	Maslow, Rogers, May	Allport, Asch
Example: Why would a person develop a mean personality?	Unconscious urges of id are not controlled.	Person has been reinforced for being mean in the past.	Person learned by watching others that you can get your way by being mean; now others expect person to be mean.	Person cannot fulfill lower needs so has not been able to strive toward potential within.	Person has traits of a mean person: is greedy, neurotic, and disagreeable.
Criticism of theory	1. Impossible to test. 2. Some ideas peculiar to Freud's time and society. 3. Generalized findings from his patients to all people. 4. Overemphasizes the unconscious.	1. Not every behavior can be learned through conditioning. 2. People are not that passive. 3. Too "cold".	1. Does not distinguish between the cause of a behavior and its consequences.	1. Many assumptions not testable; terminology is vague. 2. More of a philosophy than a science.	1. Traits not always stable across different situations. 2. Personality not really made of distinct pieces.

Descriptive Map The map on Freud's view of the structure of personality (Figure 7.2) contains the main concepts associated with his view. This map is not intended to provide an in-depth explanation of each concept; rather, it provides you with enough information to jog your memory about the details of each concept. The format of the map, however, shows you how the concepts are related to each other, which will help your recall of how the entire personality structure works together.

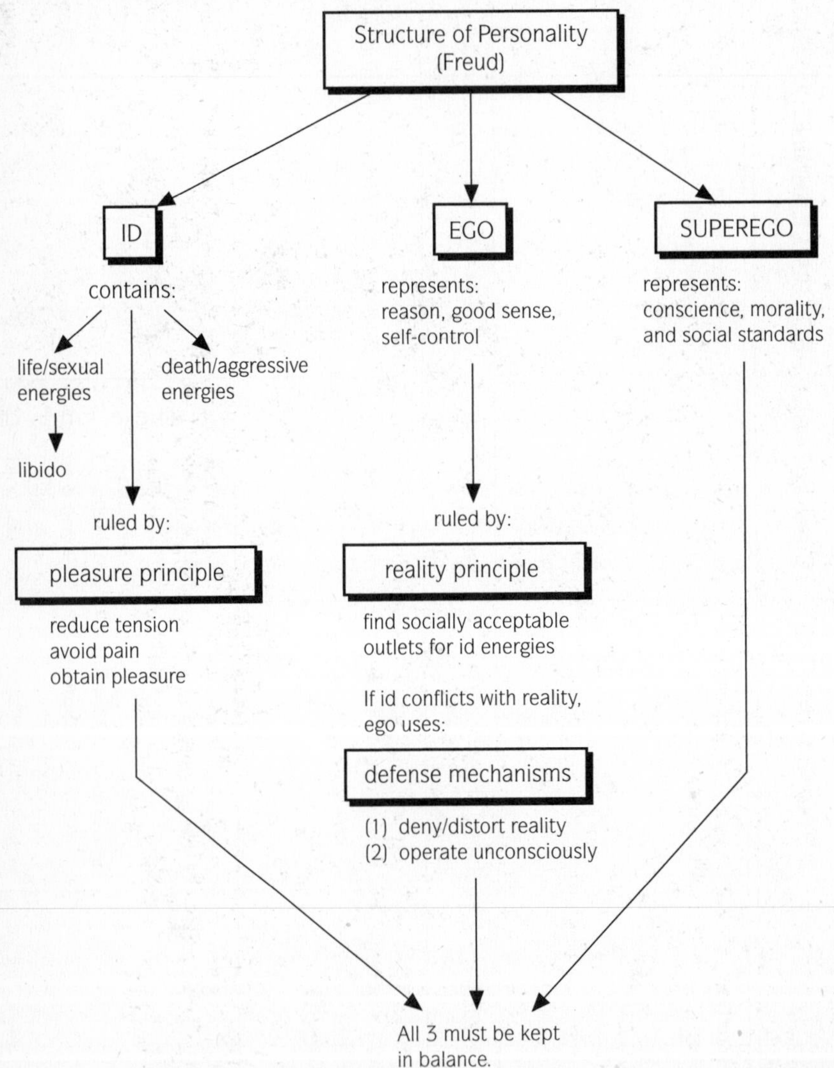

Figure 7.2 A descriptive map for Freud's view of the structure of personality

For example, you know that the three main components of personality in Freud's view are the id, ego, and superego because they are all at the same level in the map. You also know that two of the components operate according to certain principles (the id by the pleasure principle, the ego by the reality principle), and that defense mechanisms are related to the ego, rather than the id or superego. Make the layout of the map work for you. Design it so that it will optimally aid your recall. (Hint: Use vocabulary cards for each defense mechanism because there are a lot of them, and imagery will help you to remember each one.)

Web The web (Figure 7.3) that shows several strategies for effectively coping with stress just demonstrates a different way of graphically displaying information for learning. Webs are useful when you do not need to know related information in a particular order or the ideas are of equal importance.

As we mentioned in Chapter 5, it takes practice to get good at detecting what information is best studied from a map, but the strategy works well. As you examine a chapter to decide which strategies to use, look for sections that talk about a particular concept and then provide characteristics, related concepts, a series, or list. These kinds of sections will probably map well.

When you start to make a map, think about the passage's key idea, the subcategories, and the supporting details and examples. Do not try to put too much information in a map; make more maps rather than try to get all the important ideas on one page. At the other extreme, if you

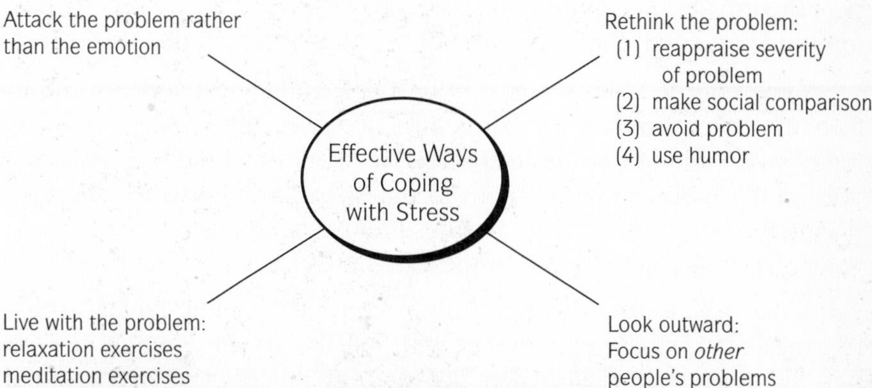

Figure 7.3 A web describing effective ways to cope with stress

only have a few words on a map, the idea is probably not as important as you first thought, and a vocabulary card or a questioning guide may be more useful.

Maps probably take more practice than the other strategies before you become proficient; however, they can be very effective. Look for whole sections in the psychology chapter you are currently reading that would map well: focus on the "big ideas."

Vocabulary Cards

In Chapter 5, we showed you how to use vocabulary cards to learn new vocabulary in psychology. You can also use cards to remember main ideas and supporting details. If you wanted to remember the three main biases in the study of personality, you could construct a card that looks like the one in Figure 7.4. On the front, write *3 main biases in seeing personality as stable.* To remind yourself which section of the text this concept is related to, write *stability vs. change* (this is the section in which it occurs in the book from which we are working) in the upper right-hand corner of the card. In the upper left-hand corner, write the page number on which this information occurs in case you want or need to refer to the text for clarification. Below the main concept, draw an image that will remind you of each bias. We chose to draw a checkerboard to remind us of patterns, an eye for **perceptual bias,** and USA to represent our possible **cultural bias.** You should draw whatever will best remind you of each bias.

On the back of the card, briefly describe the three main biases: pleasure of seeing patterns, perceptual bias, and cultural bias. Then, repeat the images. Recall from the previous chapter that consistently pairing the image with the concept will result in better recall.

Remember that as you go through the cards and overlearn the information, you can sort the cards into two piles—the terms you know really well and the ones you still need to work on. Take the cards with you so that you can study them in the spare moments that you have during the course of the day. Besides the use of imagery, one of the advantages of this strategy is that the cards are portable.

If the psychology chapter you are currently reading contains new, technical vocabulary, experiment with vocabulary cards now. Remember, the imagery is what makes this strategy much more effective than mere flash cards.

pp. 412–414 Stability vs. Change

3 main biases in seeing personality as stable

U.S.A.

(front)

(1) Pleasure of seeing patterns—string events together to create a pattern, forgetting other choices and decisions.

(2) Perceptual bias—see consistency in isolated events, not realizing it doesn't work for everyone.

(3) Cultural bias—a society or culture may value stability; may view "outsiders" from a culture that *doesn't* value stability as deviant.

U.S.A.

(back)

Figure 7.4 A sample vocabulary card to use in remembering the three main biases in the study of personality

REHEARSE, REHEARSE, REHEARSE

Making strategy materials helps you understand the information and get it into your head, but making them is not enough. Now, you have to practice what you know so that you will not forget it when you sit down to take the test. **Rehearsal,** saying information over and over again, will improve your understanding and retention of the material. Rehearsal is the key to storing information in your long-term memory. Without rehearsing it, information will only remain in your short-term memory for five to thirty seconds, and then it will disappear.

The best way to learn the material is to rehearse it out loud from your annotations and strategies. Saying the information out loud is important. You should overlearn the information by rehearsing until you are sick of hearing yourself talk. Why? How often have you gone into a test believing that you absolutely know certain information, only to find out that you have forgotten it? When you overlearn, you make it a lot less likely that you will forget the material on test day.

Do not just stare at your annotations and strategies, read them out loud over and over. Instead, overlearn and rehearse by self-testing. Self-testing forces you to be actively involved in recalling information. We are sure that you remember the importance of active involvement when it comes to memory!

When you say the information out loud, pay attention to what you are saying. Mindlessly repeating facts while your brain is engaged in considering what you are going to do this weekend is not studying. If you are not paying attention to what you are saying, you are wasting your time. Talk through the information, saying out loud what you remember. Then, check your answers against the information on your strategy materials. If you missed important material, talk your way through it again, slowly filling in the gaps. Keep rehearsing the material (main ideas and details) until you know it with little or no hesitation.

STUDY PARTNERS/GROUPS

Studying and rehearsing with one or more people from your class can be a good study strategy. Each person in a study group will have different questions, and you get the opportunity to hear information phrased differently, consider questions you had not thought of yourself, learn what material others think is most important for the upcoming test, and express your intended responses to questions to see if they make sense to others.

Another advantage to having study partners is helping each other discover mistakes and misunderstandings. It requires the same time and effort to learn the wrong material as it does to learn the right material. This unfortunate situation is easily avoided when you work in a study group because if you suggest an answer to a question and it does not agree with everyone else's understanding of the right answer, they will let you know. Study groups also break up the monotony of repeating facts and details over and over to yourself.

A word of caution with study groups: make sure you choose a study partner or group that is well informed, motivated, and serious about doing well in the class. Avoid working with people who waste time or are ill prepared.

▪

PERSONAL LEARNING QUESTIONS

Have you every worked with a study partner or group before? What were the positive and negative aspects of your experience? How can you make study partners/groups work well for you?

▪

Part of studying is creating these strategies, doing something meaningful with the information, and overlearning the information so that you can call it up easily during the test. Another part of studying is strategically planning your study time for an upcoming test and having a few strategies for different kinds of tests (essay or objective). In the next chapter, we will tell you about how to use these strategies to prepare for taking your tests.

APPLICATION EXERCISES

1. As you study your psychology chapters, try to use each one of the strategies discussed when appropriate. Determine what

information you need to know and which strategy would best help you learn the material.

2. Try all the strategies over the course of the quarter or semester, in your psychology course and other courses. It takes a while to become proficient with them. Determine which ones work best for you with different kinds of materials.
3. Ask your professor to look at your strategy materials. He or she may have some suggestions for improvement and let you know if you are studying the appropriate information.

TERMS TO KNOW

Adler
cultural bias
Freud
Horney
Jung
perceptual bias
rehearsal
Wundt

CHAPTER 8

PREPARING FOR TESTS IN PSYCHOLOGY

GETTING FOCUSED

- *Do you know how to prepare for essay tests?*
- *Do you know how to prepare for multiple choice tests?*
- *Can you construct and use a cue card?*
- *Do you use your study time wisely?*
- *How do you cope with test anxiety?*
- *How do you plan for future tests?*

■

PERSONAL LEARNING QUESTIONS

Jot down in the margin how you usually prepare for tests. Do you prepare differently for essay tests than for objective tests? If so, what are the differences?

■

Many people believe that the key to successful test preparation is to spend a lot of time studying beforehand. Generally, it is true that the more time you spend preparing for a test, the better you will do. What many people overlook, however, is that how they study is also crucial to test performance. Three or four hours of studying can yield very different results depending on how you go about studying. In this chapter, we will suggest some effective strategies for preparing for different kinds of tests. We will then provide you with information about how to take tests and how to cope with test anxiety.

HOW TO STUDY FROM YOUR STRATEGIES

In Chapter 7, we suggested how to use different strategies to study. To refresh your memory:

1. When you review your vocabulary cards, try to recall the definitions by examining the word, the subcategory, and the image before checking the meaning on the back.

2. When you study your maps, try to write them a few times from memory. Ask yourself questions based on the subcategories and lists included in the maps.

3. Your study guide is already set up for self-testing because of its format with questions on one half of the page, answers on the other. Ask yourself a question, say the answer, and check your accuracy. Have a study partner ask you the questions in a different order than you have them written on the study guide. (Remember the hazards of the serial position effect!)

4. With timelines, you can test from the date to the event or the event to the date, if you think dates are important. If dates are not important, but you need to have an overall idea of the

chronology of the development of certain theories, for example, you can summarize your timeline in paragraph form.

5. If you feel the need to review your annotations, ask questions about the material and check your annotations for the answers.

As you overlearn the information contained in your strategies, you also need to consider how you will prepare for different kinds of tests: essay and objective.

ESSAY TEST PREPARATION

Although most psychology tests tend to be objective (multiple choice, true/false, matching), you may have an instructor who wants you to be able to respond to a "big picture" psychology question in an essay. If you tend to lose most of your test points on essays or are often a victim of writer's block when you are working under timed conditions, you need to prepare yourself ahead of time and not be taken by surprise.

PORPE

A very helpful and effective strategy for essay test preparation is called PORPE.[1] PORPE stands for predict, organize, rehearse, practice, and evaluate. Here is what you do, step by step:

1. *Predict.* Several days before the test, predict a couple of possible essay questions. In order to predict well, you have to try to get inside the instructor's head and think what he or she might ask. Consider the material and the "big picture" topics in the chapters you studied. What about the lecture notes—was this information substantially different from what the text presented? If so, what are the "big picture" topics there? Are there any old tests from this course on file in the library? Remember, essay questions usually focus on the large issues and topics, not the picky little details. Try to word your questions the way essay questions are usually worded, using terms like *explain, discuss, compare and contrast, interpret, evaluate,* and *justify*.

---

[1]M. L. Simpson, "PORPE: A Writing Strategy for Studying and Learning in the Content Areas," *Journal of Reading,* 29, 1986, 407–414. Copyright by the International Reading Association.

2. *Organize.* Once you have predicted your questions, organize the material that you need to answer the questions. Perhaps you already have a map prepared for the topic. Use that. If not, gather all your information about the topic (text, cards, maps, etc.), and create a map or outline for your response to the question.

3. *Rehearse.* From your map or outline, rehearse the material out loud, over and over, until you are comfortable that you know it well and do not have to search around your brain for the main points and supporting details and examples.

4. *Practice.* Here is where the real work begins. Practice writing the answer to your question, without notes, in the amount of time you think you will have for it in class. If you have trouble answering the question, go back to step 3 and rehearse the information. If you have trouble getting the essay to "flow," go back to step 2 and work on your map or outline. Then, try to write the essay again.

5. *Evaluate.* Reread your answer and see if you included all the necessary information. Then, evaluate your response for clarity, organization, and logic. Did you use paragraphs? It is very difficult to find a student's main points if the essay is just one huge, rambling paragraph. Organize your answer. Will your instructor be able to follow your line of reasoning? Do you have sufficient support for your opinions or main points? Did you eliminate or at least reduce to a minimum any "filler"? Instructors can spot this easily, so be as direct as possible. For example, if an essay question involves Freud's life, do not write anything you can think of about Freud. Keep in mind what the question is specifically asking about Freud.

This technique works very well for preparing for essay tests. It takes time and effort, but we see a dramatic, positive difference in our students' essays when they use this strategy.

Sample Essay Response

To give you an idea of how to answer an essay question, we have written a response to this question on the topic of personality:

Are people basically good or basically evil? Answer this question from a psychoanalytic perspective, a humanistic perspective, and a behavioristic perspective.

This question requires that you understand the differences among the three main schools of thought in psychology, and then that you apply your knowledge of each school to the issue of people's inherent goodness or evil. Read the essay, and then we will analyze it.

Sample Response

Are people basically good or basically evil? In order to answer this question from a psychological perspective, you must take into consideration the psychological orientation, or school of thought, from which you are responding. The answer to this question is very different depending on whether you are taking a psychoanalytic, humanistic, or behavioristic point of view.

Freud believed that people are basically evil. When we are born, we are controlled by our id. The motivations that drive our behavior are selfish, consisting mostly of sexual desires and violent urges. According to the psychoanalytic school of thought, we only resist our evil impulses because society and especially our parents, force us to do so. From our parents' influence develops the superego, which is the moral part of us that keeps the id in check. But the id was there first. It is our true nature, and it is evil.

From a humanistic perspective, however, people are basically good. According to humanism, we are all striving to become self-actualized, which means that we are striving to reach our highest potential and highest good. The reason that some people do evil things is that they are stuck at a lower level of the hierarchy of needs, such as the safety or self-esteem needs. For example, someone who is starving may act in an evil manner to obtain food. He or she is hardly in a position to consider more aesthetic or spiritual aspects of life. But even these individuals have the potential to be good. The humanists believe that there is a basic goodness in all of us that is always working to come forth.

Behaviorists believe that people are, at their core, neither good nor evil. According to a behavioral perspective, people start out as "blank slates," and they learn to be good or bad through their experiences. When people are primarily reinforced for being good, they are primarily good. If they are primarily reinforced for being bad (for example, learning that hitting other children results in those children backing down and giving in to demands), then they are primarily bad. Skinner, one of the leaders of behaviorism, believed that if you took a group of children at birth and gave them the right reinforcements, you could make them into anything you wanted them to be—doctors, lawyers, thieves or killers. People become what they are through experiences.

In conclusion, there is little agreement among the three main psychological orientations about our true nature. It is likely that no one view is absolutely correct—each view sheds at least some light on the question.

Evaluation of Essay What makes this essay "good"? Let's start at its beginning. First, the question has been repeated and restated. It tells the reader very clearly that the issue, people's inherent goodness or evil, will be explored from three perspectives. These three perspectives will form the body of the essay. This introductory paragraph tells the reader what to expect in the rest of the essay. For you, the writer, the introductory paragraph serves as a guide—it keeps you focused on what you are going to write. Writing a clear, concise introduction will help you avoid going off on tangents later in the essay.

The second paragraph describes the psychoanalytic view of the issue. It explains concisely how the basic structures of personality dealing with goodness and evil work, how the id and superego develop and operate at opposite ends of the spectrum. Note that this paragraph deals only with the psychoanalytic view.

The third paragraph deals only with humanism's view of the question. It explains the concepts of self-actualization and the hierarchy of needs and how evil can develop in basically good people. An example is used to clarify the explanation.

The fourth paragraph focuses on behaviorism, and specific examples help to describe the concept.

Finally, a concluding statement summarizes the situation, that different schools of thought take radically different views on the subject of human nature.

This essay is not necessarily the most creative or insightful response ever written on the subject, but essays written in class, in a timed situation, rarely need to be works of art. Rather, you are expected to demonstrate solid knowledge of the topic and clarity in expressing your knowledge. Even in a timed test, you do need to write legibly, spell correctly, and use correct grammar and clear sentence structure. If you practice possible essay questions ahead of time, you will become more skilled at answering questions directly and concisely.

Sample Essay Questions

To give you an idea of what an essay question on an introductory psychology test might look like, we have provided you with one sample question in each of the seven general areas of psychology. You will find these sample questions in Appendix 1, one under each of the seven areas. It is unlikely that you will find one of these exact questions on your test because there are many topics for essays that your instructor can choose. However, these examples will give you an idea of what format an essay question might take, and they should make it easier for you to predict what specific questions your instructor will ask.

TIPS ON MULTIPLE CHOICE QUESTIONS

The most common type of question you are likely to see on a psychology test is multiple choice. Introductory psychology classes tend to be quite large. If a class has 75, 150, or maybe even 600 students in it, the instructor simply cannot grade short answer and essay questions. Multiple choice, true/false, and matching questions are efficient to use.

Just to get you in the multiple choice mood, let's do one:

> *You are bitten by a dog. You must now undergo a series of painful injections to avoid getting rabies. The doctor cleans your skin with rubbing alcohol before giving you each injection. You now become anxious every time you smell rubbing alcohol. This phenomenon is an example of:*
>
> *a. observational learning.*
> *b. classical conditioning.*
> *c. operant conditioning.*
> *d. psychoanalysis.*

(The correct answer is b; the example demonstrates learning by association, or classical conditioning.)

When you read a multiple choice question, do not immediately look at the possible choices. Cover up the answers and first see if you can come up with the answer on your own. If you know the answer, then check to see if it is there. This way, you avoid being seduced or confused by wrong answers that sound good. One of the answers to a multiple choice question is correct; the other three or four answers are put there to sound correct. Sometimes, a wrong answer can sound correct because it is the "right" answer to another question.

If you have to guess, there are some strategies that can increase your chances of guessing correctly.

1. If one answer is longer than the rest, consider it. Right answers often require a lot of words to be properly phrased:

   Jung's "collective unconscious" is best described as:

   a. the part of the unconscious mind that forms dreams.
   b. the part of the unconscious mind that holds painful memories.
   c. the total of all things in your unconscious mind.
   d. memories in your unconscious mind that have been passed down from your ancient ancestors.

   (The correct answer is d.)

2. If two answers look or sound similar, narrow your choice to one of those two answers:

   According to Freud, which structure in personality is concerned with morality?

   a. Id
   b. Superego
   c. Alter ego
   d. Oedipus

   (The correct answer is b.)

3. If the answers to a question involve a range of answers that are in some sort of order, consider an answer in the middle of the range:

   According to Piaget, a child is in the stage of concrete operations from ages:

   a. birth to 2 years.
   b. 2 to 7 years.
   c. 7 to 11 years.
   d. 11 years and up.

   (The correct answer is b.)

4. Rule out answers that do not sound right. If an answer is phrased badly or combines awkwardly with the sentence, it is probably not the correct answer:

   Multiple personality is a:

   a. dissociative disorder.
   b. schizophrenic disorder.
   c. mood disorder.
   d. anxiety disorder.

   (In this example, you would rule out choice d, because it would read "Multiple personality is a anxiety disorder." The correct answer is a.)

Keep two other things in mind when answering multiple choice and other objective test questions. First, if you are guessing at an answer, never change that guess unless you remember new information that makes it clear that another answer is correct (or is more likely to be correct). When taking a guess, your first impulse tends to be your best. Why? Probably because that little voice that is your unconscious mind sometimes helps you out. You may feel that you are completely guessing, but first impressions are sometimes guided by a part of your mind that remembers something of which your conscious mind is not aware. We do not know for sure that that is what is going on. It is an educated guess based on something we do know. When people change their guesses, they are far more likely to change from a right answer to a wrong answer than from a wrong answer to a right one. (This may vary from person to person, so learn to be a good student of your own test-taking patterns.)

The other thing that you should keep in mind when answering objective test questions is this: if you are taking a test that is going to be scored by a machine, be sure to erase completely when you change an answer. We know, you have been hearing this since first grade, but it is amazing how many times answers are marked wrong because of failures to properly erase. Bring big, clean erasers and use them!

CUE CARD: THE FINAL STEP

As you rehearse the information and prepare for essays or objective questions, you will need to rely less and less on what you have written in your strategies. Weed out the maps and vocabulary cards you already know well and focus on the material that is still giving you trouble. When you are comfortable (or close to it) with most of the information, you are ready for the final step: a cue card.

The night before the test (or even two nights before, if you are really serious), get together all of your information: text, annotations, maps, vocabulary cards, timelines, study guides, and whatever else you have devised. Then, reduce all this information down to one 3 X 5 cue card. This does not require that you write every single piece of information in the world's tiniest print. Narrow down your information to the major concepts.

Sample Cue Card

For example, let's say that you are tested every Friday in your psychology class, one chapter a week plus lecture notes. This week's test covers the chapter on memory and forgetting. Your cue card might look like the one in Figure 8.1. Notice how just the major concepts are listed. No definitions of terms and not much elaboration on the "big ideas." Definitions and other details should be in your head by now because you have rehearsed them and worked with them in the various strategies. To use this one card, you look at a major concept and try to recall everything you know about it. Just looking at the word should "call up" your schema for it. Say out loud all the information you know about that concept, or have a study partner quiz you on each concept.

Memory—learning persisting over time

flashbulb memories—clear mems. of emotional moments

Mem. as info proc.–3 steps: encode, store, retrieve

Sensory register–info coming into senses: iconic (Sperling), echoic

Memory consists of encoding, storage, & retrieval

1–*ENCODING*—how? visual, acoustic, semantic (can be combined)

2 types mem. storage–STM/LTM

STM–brief duration, acoustic, limited capacity
LTM–permanent, semantic, unlimited capacity

encoding can be automatic or effortful
amt. remembered depends on time spent learning

serial position effect–first & last items on a list remembered best

Effective info processing–use meaning cues, imagery, & organization

2–*STORAGE*–capacity
STM–7+/-2 (Miller); acoustic remembered better than iconic; adults better than kids
LTM–limitless, but how precise? (Penfield, Loftus)

Declarative mems–events, names
Procedural mems–how to do something
Decl. & proc. processed differently

3–*RETRIEVAL*–recall, recognition, relearning

Retrieval cues–the more & better learned the cues, the more access to the memory.

1–context effects–remember better when in same context as when learned the material

2–moods/mems–state dependent memory–recall better when in same mood as when learned the material; affects whole outlook; episodic memory. Affects encoding and retrieval.

3–memory construction–alterations, confabulation. Affects encoding & retrieval. (Loftus–misleading info can affect recall.)

4–metacognition–awareness of own thinking processes. Self-testing increases effectiveness of active rehearsal and metacognition.

FORGETTING–occurs at any stage (encoding, storage, retrieval)

Interference–proactive (old info interferes w/ learning new info); retroactive (new info interferes w/old info)

To improve memory–rehearse, be active learner, make learning meaningful, use mnemonics and other cues, minimize interference, consider mood and context, self-test

Figure 8.1 A sample cue card for studying a chapter on memory and forgetting

DISTRIBUTING YOUR STUDY TIME

Remember in Chapter 6 when we briefly mentioned that it is more effective to spread out your study time over a few days than to put in many hours the night before the test? Now that you know a variety of test preparation strategies, it is time to figure out how to schedule enough time to make good use of the strategies you have devised and how to distribute your time and avoid cramming.

Let's say that today is Friday, October 16, and you have a midterm in psychology coming up in one week on Friday, October 23. The test covers four textbook chapters and the lecture notes that go with those chapters. Let's also say that you have already read and annotated the chapters, and you have already made your strategy materials. The following study plan assumes that you have already put in the necessary reading and strategy construction, and you are all set to study.

Examine the study plan in Table 8.1. Look at this plan in detail.

TABLE 8.1 STUDY PLAN FOR PSYCHOLOGY MIDTERM

WHEN?	WHAT I'M GOING TO DO	WHERE?	FOR HOW LONG?
Fri., 10/16 9-10:30 a.m.	Study Ch. 5. Get chapter, maps, cards, etc., together. Rehearse material out loud. Predict and answer possible test questions.	dorm rm	1 1/2 hours
Sun., 10/18 7-8:30 p.m.	Rev. Ch. 5. Study Ch. 6. Get chapter, maps, cards, etc., together. Rehearse material. Predict and answer possible test questions.	library	1 1/2 hours
Mon., 10/19 8:30-10:30 a.m.	Rev. Ch. 5, 6. Study Ch. 7. Get chapter, maps, cards, etc., together. Rehearse material. Predict and answer possible test questions.	library	2 hours
Tues., 10/20 7-9 p.m.	Rev. Ch. 5, 6, 7. Study Ch. 8. Get chapter, maps, cards together. Rehearse material. Predict and answer possible test questions.	dorm rm	2 hours
Wed., 10/21 8:30-10:30 a.m.	Review all chapters. Rehearse. Predict and answer possible essay question. Work w/study partner for 30 minutes.	library	2 hours
Thurs., 10/22 9-10:30 p.m.	Make 3x5 cue card. Rehearse.	dorm rm	1 1/2 hours
Fri., 10/23 11 a.m.-noon	TEST!	classrm	1 hour

Adapted from M. L. Simpson and S. L. Nist, "PLAE: A Model for Independent Learning," *Journal of Reading,* 28, 1984, 218–223. Copyright by the International Reading Association.

Spread Out Study Time

First, notice that study time is spread out over the whole week, with the exception of Saturday, but it is never more than two hours at a time. Both morning and evening times are slotted in. Try to study during the same time periods each day, whenever that may be.

List Specific Tasks

Next, look at what you accomplish each time you sit down to study. You do not try to plow through all four chapters, rereading or rewriting. Instead, you have a specific task to accomplish during each study period. Just as you divided up reading assignments for annotating so that you were not slogging through the whole thing in one sitting, you divide up the material for studying. Also, each task is now specific. You do not simply say "study." You say that you are going to get together all the material related to one chapter, rehearse it, predict possible test questions, and try to answer them. Notice that these are active strategies that involve you in self-testing, rather than just rereading.

Review During Each Study Session

Each time you sit down to study for this test, you review the material you studied during the last session. This review should only take about 15–30 minutes, depending on the amount of material. Reviewing should be just as active as studying, including rehearsing, self-testing, and writing. Then, you start in on the next chapter.

The Day or Two Before the Test

By two nights before the test, you should be reviewing all of the material and predicting and answering possible essay questions. You might also want a study partner to test you (although this can be done earlier and more often, if you find that it works well for you). By the night before (or earlier, if time permits), you should be putting together your cue card and testing yourself or working with a study partner.

Obviously, you will need to adjust your study plan to your own schedule. Study when you are most alert, and allow time for doing other class assignments. The example that we have given you suggests the basics of an effective way to schedule study time. Remember, following this type of schedule depends on doing the groundwork (reading, annotating, developing strategies) ahead of time.

TAKING THE TEST

▪

PERSONAL LEARNING QUESTIONS

How do you feel when you enter a classroom to take a test? Consider your state of mind and degree of preparation.

▪

Once you get control of your study strategies, all that is left is to actually take the test. If you get overly anxious during tests, we have some suggestions for how to reduce anxiety in this chapter. If you have just a normal amount of anxiety, do not be concerned: a little anxiety will make you alert and psych you up for the test.

Be Early and Be Prepared

On the day of the test, try to get to the classroom a little earlier than usual so that you are not running in at the last minute. It is more relaxing to be a little early and take your time getting comfortable. If you spend your last minutes before a test trying to calm down and get yourself oriented, you will not be in the best frame of mind to take the test. Always bring two sharpened pencils with good erasers—if you have essays or seemingly several hundred thousand little circles to bubble in on answer sheets, you will probably need that second pencil. Avoid using the time to keep sharpening one pencil over and over.

Calm Your Thoughts

Now that you are at your seat early, with two #2 pencils, get yourself mentally prepared for the exam. Calm your thoughts if you can. Breathe deeply and regularly. In anxiety-producing situations, we often breathe shallowly and rapidly. Get lots of oxygen to your brain to help it work effectively.

Preview the Entire Test

When the test is handed to you, and as you are breathing deeply, take the time to look over the entire test. How long is it? How many points is each question worth? Is one section worth a lot more than another? How much time do you have to complete the test? If an essay question is included that is worth a lot of points, try to save about 20 or more minutes to answer it. While you are looking over the questions, jot down any information that you will need that you are afraid you might forget. Then you do not have to worry about that information going anywhere; it is right there for you.

You are ready to begin. Look for some questions you know you can answer with no difficulty, and answer them to build your confidence.

What's that? We have not accurately described your experience of test taking because we have not mentioned icy terror and slick, sweaty palms? We are getting to that.

TECHNIQUES FOR COPING WITH TEST ANXIETY

You may have no trouble with test anxiety. There is an art to being anxious that only some of us are unfortunate enough to perfect. If you do not get overly anxious or fearful before or during tests, skip this section. If you do get anxious before tests (or, for that matter, if you get anxious before or during anything), read on.

Anxiety is unpleasant. Test anxiety is worse because it is unpleasant *and* it occurs in a situation that affects your grade. If you get a little tense before an exam, do not worry. A little anxiety can actually work to your advantage by making you alert. But if you get so anxious that your pen keeps falling out of your hand because of the sweat on your palms, it is obviously hurting your grade. What can you do about it? There is not a clear-cut answer for that question. There are several techniques that are supposed to work, but the truth is, they may work for you, and they may not.

Anxiety is tricky. We only have a limited amount of control over how nervous we become in a particular situation. As you may be well aware, it is possible to be anxious about becoming anxious, and resisting anxiety only makes it worse. We know this statement is not very comforting to hear if you tend to blank out when you sit down to take a test, but we may be able to give you some insight into your anxiety.

Here are a few techniques that often help to reduce anxiety. Remember, you do not need to reduce your anxiety to a point at which you are totally relaxed. You just have to drop the anxiety level to a point well below sheer panic.

Be Prepared for the Test

Although this suggestion is not exactly what you were expecting to read as a cure for test anxiety, it really is your best defense. You are most likely to panic during a test if you are worried about failing. If you walk in prepared, you will be more confident and less likely to be anxious.

Do a Relaxation Exercise

Close your eyes and begin taking deep, even breaths. Now, focus on relaxing your toes. When your toes are relaxed, focus on relaxing your feet. Then, relax your ankles, calves, knees, thighs, and so on up your body until you are fully relaxed.

Anxiety is very much a bodily sensation. It may start in your mind, but it is the symptoms of shallow breathing, muscle tension, "butterflies," and sweating that make anxiety really unpleasant. You cannot be tense and relaxed at the same time, so if you do this relaxation exercise before (or during) the test, it can short-circuit much of the anxiety.

Relaxation is a popular **behavioristic** technique for reducing all types of anxiety. The focus of the treatment is on the behavior (the symptoms), not the thoughts that lead to the symptoms (in this case, the thoughts of failing the test).

Put the Test in Perspective

When you are 80 years old looking back over your life, chances are slim that you will think, "Yes, things would have been different in my life if I had not blown that intro psych exam 62 years ago." Tests are important, but keep a sense of perspective. The difference between a B and a C (or between a C and a D, for that matter) in one course turns out to be minuscule in your overall grade point average by the time you are a senior. You are taking one test in one course. Your academic career does not ride on it.

One of the reasons people get anxious before tests is because their self-image is overly invested in their grades. They believe that failing a test means more than a low average in psychology class; it means they are losers and overall failures. Do not get locked into that mentality if you can avoid it. Give yourself a break. A bad test grade is a bad test grade. It gives you feedback that you are not understanding the material, or you are not preparing well for the exams. It is not a testament of your self-worth. Remember, the key to success is perseverance. If you keep getting up, brushing yourself off, and forging ahead, you will do well in the long run, where it really matters.

In contrast to the previous technique, which was behavioral, this one is a **cognitive** technique. You are trying to intercept the thoughts that lead to anxiety, not the symptoms of anxiety themselves.

When All Else Fails, Accept the Anxiety

The main thing to keep in mind about anxiety is not to get anxious about being anxious. You do not have much control over being anxious. The more you try to resist anxiety, the more anxious you become. Do not walk into a test thinking, "Oh, no! I'm so anxious, I'm going to faint!" or "I have to stop being anxious." If you are anxious, and you have tried to calm down using one of the techniques that we have mentioned, but you cannot, the best thing to do is to accept it. There is nothing unnatural or terrible about anxiety. Think to yourself, "Okay, I am really nervous. It is not going to help to worry about it, so I'll just be nervous and take the test." If you do not try to resist, the anxiety will likely stay at a manageable level.

Something even more interesting may happen. If you accept the fact that you are anxious, and you let the anxiety go, you may find that the anxiety has melted away. Fear is a funny thing. If you resist it, it owns you. If you accept it as a natural part of being human and forge ahead regardless, it loses much of its power over you.

PLANNING FOR FUTURE TESTS

When your test is graded and returned to you, you may think, "Well, that's that! Another test over with!" Whether or not you did well on the test, you can learn a great deal from your mistakes and successes. Instead of glancing at the grade and stashing the test in your notebook, take a closer look at your work.[2]

What Types of Questions Did You Miss?

What kinds of questions did you miss? Multiple choice, true/false, short answer or essay? If you missed more true/false questions than multiple

---

[2] M. L. Simpson, "PLAE: A Model for Planning Successful Independent Learning," *Journal of Reading*, 28, 1986, 218–223. Copyright by the International Reading Association.

choice, for example, why? What was it about the wording of the true/false questions that threw you off? Similarly, if you did well on the multiple choice and true/false questions and poorly on the short answer and essay questions, this pattern indicates that you will need to spend extra work on expressing your responses clearly or organizing your thoughts or simply knowing the information well enough to be able to state it rather than simply reacting to or recognizing it.

Why Did You Miss Those Questions?

Another important area to examine is the reason why you missed the questions you did. If you missed all the questions on the difference between classical and operant conditioning, for example, but did well on most other areas on the test, you know that you need to go back and study that information again if you will be retested on this material on the midterm or final exam. Did you miss questions about definitions of concepts? If so, this pattern indicates that you need a strategy that focuses on vocabulary, such as vocabulary cards. Did it seem that nearly all the options could be the correct answer? Then you probably did not know the information as well as you thought you did, and you will need to spend more and/or better time studying for future tests. Look for trends in your errors; then, spend time making sure you won't make those errors again.

Going over tests is especially important if you will be taking a cumulative final exam (one that covers all the material from the entire semester, rather than one that tests only the material you have learned since the last test). Not only do you want to avoid getting the same questions wrong the second time around, but it is a good bet that the final exam will emphasize the same material as the first test did on that area. The first test indicated what material your instructor thought was most important for you to know. It is likely that your instructor will still consider that material highly important when it is time for the final exam.

▪

Personal Learning Questions

Examine your latest multiple choice or essay test results in psychology or any other course you are taking. What kinds of mistakes did you make? Were there any patterns to your errors? What can you learn from this experience to improve for the next test?

▪

A Sample Introductory Psychology Test

It might be useful for you to view an introductory psychology test. One of the authors' actual tests is provided in Appendix 2. Keep in mind that different instructors test in different ways. Some instructors include mostly broad questions that test whether or not you understand the major concepts. Others ask many questions that require you to know exact details, like psychologists' names or the names and functions of all of the parts of the eye.

Some of the questions on our sample exam concern material that we have not gone over in the course of this book. Remember, the purpose of reading this book is not to give you all the psychology information you need to ace your test, but to give you the tools to learn psychology efficiently and effectively.

APPLICATION EXERCISES

1. Make a study plan for your next psychology test. Be sure to include enough study time distributed over a few or several days, and plenty of review.
2. Make a cue card for your next psychology test.
3. If taking tests makes you very anxious, try some of the strategies we discussed above. Be aware of how you feel and whether the strategies alleviate any amount of stress.
4. If you anticipate an essay question on your next psychology test, use PORPE to predict possible questions and practice responding.

TERMS TO KNOW

behavioristic
cognitive

CHAPTER 9

ALL THE OTHER PARTS OF YOUR LIFE

GETTING FOCUSED

- *What are your strategies for being happy?*

▪

PERSONAL LEARNING QUESTIONS

**Take a few moments to think about this question:
Are you happy?**

▪

We have talked about what it helps to know about psychology as you enter the class and about ways to improve your memory and your reading, study, and test-taking habits, but there are other issues to consider as well.

Most learned people will tell you that all things and ideas in life are interconnected. Everything in your life has an effect on everything else in your life. You do not go to classes and study in a vacuum; the rest of your life influences your college career. For example, if you are lonely, having problems in a relationship, or running out of money, it is hard to concentrate on your studies. Larger problems may make your classes seem so insignificant that you have a difficult time caring about your grades.

To be a good student, it helps to be at peace in the other aspects of your life. Because this book is about studying and psychology, it seems appropriate to say something about what psychologists know about getting and staying happy. We certainly do not claim that we can erase any and all difficulties that you have in your life in a few pages (or in a thousand pages, for that matter). We can, however, offer you some thoughts and insights that might point you in the direction of happiness.

THE ART (AND SCIENCE) OF HAPPINESS

▪

PERSONAL LEARNING QUESTIONS

Jot down in the margin a few things that you think make you happy.

▪

Happiness can be defined as the judgment you make about the overall quality of your experience. It is more than just being in a good mood although mood does affect happiness. The following are some of the central points in the art of being happy.

Remove Your Expectations of What *Should* Make You Happy

Many of the things you listed do not, in general, make people happier. Most people believe, for instance, that if they had more money, they would be happier. Researchers surveyed people who had recently won large sums of money in the lottery, and found that they were no happier than you or I.[1] Many people find this hard to believe, but it is true.

Unless we lack money to buy food and other basic necessities, money provides a temporary jolt of pleasure, and then it is over. Imagine that you want to buy a little red sports car. You often think about how happy you would be if you had that car, and you picture yourself driving down the highway in it, as if you were in a commercial. Then one day, you get the car. That first ride in it is completely thrilling and satisfying. But, by the fiftieth ride, you probably do not get the same rush of enjoyment. By that time, it may be just a car to you, just a way to get from place to place. We get used to things, and when we do, we need just a little more to get the rush. Did you ever wonder why a billionaire is still trying to make more money? Because she or he can never have enough. It is like an addiction.

Pleasure and Happiness Are Not the Same

We are not saying that money and the things it can buy are not good. They provide convenience and comfort, but they do not provide happiness, and the two should not be confused. You will never get enough pleasure in your life to be happy continuously.

Which will make you happier? Good health? An education? A great job? Everyone wants good health, and most people want an education and a good job. These are also things we tend to get used to and then not notice anymore. Remember the study of the lottery winners we mentioned before? Those same researchers also talked to a group of people who had recently been paralyzed in an accident.[2] The accident survivors were slightly less happy than the lottery winners, but just slightly. It does not seem to make sense, does it? Happiness is obviously much different than we think it is.

People who have great jobs are no happier than people with not-so-great jobs. Again, this finding does not seem to make sense. It would seem that if you spend eight hours a day at a job, you would be happier if you like that job than if you do not. Think of a time when you worked at a job that you did not like. How did you feel when you got off work? Your free time was sweet, wasn't it? You really enjoyed

---

[1]P. Brickman, D. Coates, and R. Janoff-Buman, "Lottery Winners and Accident Victims: Is Happiness Relative?" *Journal of Personality and Social Psychology,* 36, 1978, 917–927.
[2]Ibid.

getting home and putting your feet up or going out with your friends. Now, think of a time when you were not working for a while. You enjoyed the free time, and there was more of it, but it probably was not quite as good as the free time after the tough job.

We have a peculiar way of balancing our life situations so that, in general, we are equally happy whether we are starving students living three to a room or wealthy doctors with two homes. Again, there are limits and exceptions. For example, if you are literally starving, or if you are dying, the situation will affect your happiness, but this is only true in the case of extreme misfortune.

The point is, improving your life situation will make you more comfortable, but it will not give you long-term happiness. The belief that your happiness depends on your life situation is a subtle way of saying that people can only be happy when things are the way they want them to be. The problem with this belief is that things are rarely the way we want them to be. An unalterable fact of life is that bad things happen from time to time. If we have to wait for our lives to be just right in order for us to be happy, we will spend our lives waiting.

There is certainly nothing wrong with trying to improve your lot in life, but do not expect that getting that job, that grade, or that car will be the key to your happiness. It is not, and if you insist on believing that it is, you will always be disappointed. If you have illusions about what happiness is, you will have trouble staying happy for long. Long-term happiness is more about your approach to life than what happens to you in your life.

▪

PERSONAL LEARNING QUESTIONS

Jot down some recent examples of times when you were feeling truly happy. What were you doing? Were you walking in the woods, playing basketball with friends, listening to music? Now, jot down what was going on in your head during those times.

▪

Stay in the Present, Not in Your Head

Chances are, your mind is not racing with thoughts. We would bet that your thoughts are slow and that you are not paying much attention to them. You are probably focused on your reading and are not thinking about what is going on around you. You are just experiencing it. Put another way, you are listening to your world rather than talking to it.

Happiness takes place in the present moment, and your greatest obstacle to staying in the present is your own thoughts.

Most of our thoughts fit into one of three categories: (1) thoughts about the past, (2) thoughts about the future, and (3) thoughts about how we wish things were right now. Go ahead, think a thought. See if it does not fit into one of these three categories. Once in a while, we have a thought like, "I'm going to eat lunch now," which is aimed at the present moment, but for the most part we think about things that are not in the present. Do you see the connection? Happiness takes place in the present, and most of our thoughts drag us out of the present.

Enjoy the Present Moment

You absolutely cannot stop your thoughts. Try not to think of anything for the next 30 seconds. It is not possible. But if you make an effort to enjoy the present moment, whether that moment involves walking in the woods or washing dirty dishes (or studying), your thoughts will fade into the background where they belong. This is called being **mindful,** aware of where you are and what you are doing at all times. Be mindful, be in the moment, and stay out of your head.

It is not easy to be mindful. Our thoughts are constantly pulling us out of the present moment and back into our heads. But if you keep reminding yourself to stay mindful, to pay attention to what you are doing, what you are eating, or hearing, or smelling, you will begin to spend more and more time in the present. More time spent in the present means more time spent being happy.

Remember earlier we said that all things and ideas are interconnected? Here is how these first two strategies for happiness are interconnected: If you believe that money, for example, will make you happier, you will spend a lot of your time thinking about getting money. When you think about having more money, you are not in the present, you are fantasizing about how you wish the present were. Therefore, you have little chance of being happy at this moment.

Keep Your Life Simple

We have a tendency to believe that "more is better," that the more filled our lives are, the happier we will be. Having a lot of "stuff," a lot of obligations, and a lot of plans offers us much to think about, so we are constantly being pulled out of the present. Let's say, for example, that you were to purchase that new sports car we mentioned earlier. Do you think you would be concerned about making the payments each month? Would you park it way out in the parking lot to avoid having it scratched, and then still worry? Would you avoid driving it on dirt roads to keep it from getting dirty? Would you have to remember to turn on an alarm each time you left it for fear of it being stolen? If you are answering "yes" to some of these questions, you can probably see how easily material objects can add complication to our lives.

Keep Your Life Uncluttered

We can do many small things to keep our lives simple. In Chapter 1, we talked about the benefits of keeping your study area uncluttered. This is one way to simplify your life. Do not let clutter build up around you in your home, apartment, or dormitory room. Another common complication in life is finances, especially debt. Try to buy as little as possible on credit. Buy something only when you have the money to pay for it.

Another area where you might simplify your life is in your daily schedule of obligations. You certainly do not want to overdo simplifying your life to the point that you have nothing to do and no friends, but choose only activities and obligations that you truly want to do or that you think are truly important to do. Avoid setting up a schedule that requires you to race from one obligation to the next from the time you wake up until the time you go to bed. Here we have another connection between two strategies: it is difficult to remember to be mindful if you are always in a hurry. It is an old cliché, but there is wisdom in the advice, "take time to stop and smell the roses."

Gandhi was a great spiritual leader of India. When he died, he owned only eyeglasses, clothing, a walking stick, and a statue of the "see no evil, hear no evil, speak no evil" monkeys. Yet most would argue that Gandhi died a happy man. We are not suggesting you give away all of your possessions and join a monastery, but do strive to keep your life uncomplicated.

Enjoy the Simple Pleasures

Another way to keep your life simple is to work at appreciating the pleasure that simple things can give you. Often, we focus our full attention only on the "big" pleasures in life such as a new relationship, a new car, a vacation to Hawaii. Focusing only on the big pleasures can lead us to overlook the simple pleasures in our lives, such as eating, taking a walk, taking a bath, smelling flowers, or taking a nap. The advantage that simple pleasures have over big pleasures is that we usually have more control over simple pleasures. We can enjoy them whenever we want to.

This is rarely the case with big pleasures. Most of us cannot buy a new sports car every year or move to Hawaii permanently. Research has shown that having many small "ups" in your life is what brings about long-term happiness. Big "ups" seem to lead to short-term rushes of pleasure, but they do little to increase the overall pleasure of life.

There is an ancient Eastern saying that at first seems nonsensical, but in light of what we know about the effects of complications on our happiness, it makes more sense. The saying is: "Less is better than more."

▪

PERSONAL LEARNING QUESTIONS

How simple or cluttered is your life right now? What steps can you take to simplify your schedule?

▪

Keep Your Body Healthy

"Wait a minute," you say. "You just finished telling me that being healthy does not make me any happier. What's the deal?" This is a bit contradictory. It is true that a person who suffers from health problems or disabilities can be just as happy as someone who does not. In general, however, differences in happiness tend to occur between people who exercise and people who do not, regardless of the existence of medical problems. Aerobic exercise (jogging, biking, aerobics) appears to lead to (slightly) greater happiness.[3] We would suggest that this finding goes back to the notion that all things are interconnected (all things go back to the notion that all things are interconnected!). Your body influences your mind, just as your mind influences your body. A fit body helps bring about a fit mind.

---

[3]E. Diener, "Subjective Well-being." *Psychological Bulletin,* 95, 1984, 542–575.

▪

PERSONAL LEARNING QUESTIONS

Do you take the time to exercise? If not, what kind of exercise would you find enjoyable? Consider when you can exercise and with whom.

▪

Invest Time in Closeness with Others

People who have close relationships are happier than people who do not. It is not the number but the quality of those friendships that leads to happiness. If your relationships with friends and family are deep and lasting, you will be happier. Spending time developing your relationships with others is worthwhile. The title of a classic textbook in social psychology, *The Social Animal,* tells the whole story. Humans are, by nature, very reliant on interaction with others. We are social animals. We do not thrive in isolation.

One painful example of how important it is to be close to others involves infants who grow up in isolation. As you will read in, perhaps, the child development chapter of your psychology textbook, for years many infants without parents were put in institutions where they had no contact with people except when they were fed or changed. They spent all day lying in a crib with no one to hold them or play with them. These children did not develop normally. Not only were they very small and sickly, but most ended up mentally and emotionally disturbed as well.[4] Their eyes were empty. What psychologists concluded from this sad situation is that from an early age people need not only food and shelter, they need the support and companionship of other people. The companionship of others is one of the only things we do need in our lives to be happy. We do not need money, intelligence, prestige, or good looks. We just need food, shelter, air to breathe, other people, and the "right" approach to life.

Not surprisingly, research has found that being outgoing also leads to happiness.[5] If you are the type of person who is at ease with others and who feels comfortable reaching out to others, you will be happier. The

---

[4]J. Bowlby, *Attachment,* Vol. I of *Attachment and Loss.* (New York: Basic Books, 1969).

[5]P. T. Costa and R. R. McCrae, "Influence of Extroversion and Neuroticism on Subjective Well-Being," *Journal of Personality and Social Psychology,* 38, (1980), 668–678.

problem here is that being outgoing is to some extent genetic. For example, twins who are reared apart tend to be similar in how outgoing they are.[6] Although each of us differs in the degree to which we feel comfortable being outgoing, all of us can benefit from greater efforts to reach out to others.

▪

PERSONAL LEARNING QUESTIONS

Are you outgoing? If not, how can you encourage yourself to become a little more outgoing?

▪

Be Optimistic

This point does not need much explanation. Optimistic people are happy people. We are sure that this statement is not a revelation to you. If you are hopeful, if you see the bright side of things, you will be happier. Be aware of how you look at the world. If you are not optimistic, work at identifying and eliminating pessimistic patterns in your thinking. In psychology, this correction is called **cognitive retraining.**

Whenever you have a pessimistic thought, such as "I'm no good at tests," follow up consciously with an optimistic thought, such as "Yes, I am good at tests, I just did not do too well on this particular one." At first, this kind of self-talk will feel very forced, but after a while you can develop the habit and replace your pessimistic thoughts. One note of caution. You have spent years developing a habitual way of thinking, and you are not going to change this way of thinking in a few weeks. Cognitive retraining takes time and perseverance.

Be Spiritual

Happy people generally have a strong spiritual thread running through their lives. For different people, spirituality can mean different things. Some follow an organized religious tradition. Others follow a more individual path. It is not even a religious path for some.

---

[6]M. W. Eysenck, *Happiness: Facts and Myths* (London: Erlbaum Associated, 1990).

In a general sense, being spiritual means carrying with you a sense of how awesome life is. Spiritual people go about their day-to-day activities with a feeling that all that they do and see is sacred.

Carl Jung, a famous psychologist, once said that a life without meaning is worthless. Spirituality gives life meaning. If you have some spiritual path that you are committed to, invest it with more energy and make it more central in your life. If you have no sense of spirituality, we suggest you consider weaving a spiritual dimension into your life. This does not necessarily mean you must find some specific doctrine to "believe." Spirituality takes many forms.

▪

PERSONAL LEARNING QUESTIONS

What does "spirituality" mean to you? How do you think you can infuse your daily life with a meaningful spirituality?

▪

Persevere

Our final word on happiness is that if you want to be a happy person, make it a conscious priority in your life. All of us want to be happy, but some work harder than others to make it a reality. If you want to be significantly happier than you are now, you must make a commitment. The commitment is that you will strive to be happier, and that you will put time and energy into it. Make a commitment now, not later, not when you have everything you need in order to be happy, because that time will never come. Something will always hold you back in your life situation if you allow it. Strive to be happy now.

THE END IS THE BEGINNING

The key to all of this information is not to leave it in the book. It is of no use to you if you do not use it. If you use what you have learned in this book, you will do better in your psychology class, and you will be a better student in general. We realize that using your new knowledge involves effort and a change in your usual learning/studying habits. You will have to decide how important it is to you to be a good student. Choose wisely!

In a sense, this is the end because you are about to finish this book. In another sense, it is the beginning because you can now begin applying what you have learned. Good luck! Now, go ace your psychology class... and strive to be happy, no matter what grade you earn.

THE ART OF HAPPINESS

1. Remove your expectations of what *should* make you happy.
2. Stay in the present, not in your head.
3. Keep your life simple.
4. Keep your body healthy.
5. Invest time in closeness with others.
6. Be optimistic.
7. Be spiritual.
8. Persevere.

APPLICATION EXERCISES

1. After reading this chapter, consider what you think are the sources of happiness and unhappiness in your life.
2. Where are your thoughts most of the time? In the past, present, or future? How can you strive to live in the present, responsibly?
3. Examine your daily schedule. How can you simplify your daily life?

TERMS TO KNOW

cognitive retraining
happiness
mindful

APPENDIX 1

KEY CONCEPTS FOR THE SEVEN AREAS OF PSYCHOLOGY

Below, you will find (1) several important concepts and examples for each of the seven areas of psychology; and (2) one sample essay question for each area. Notice that some of the questions are very broad, such as the personality question, while some are more specific, such as the general experimental question.

IMPORTANT CONCEPTS IN BIOLOGICAL PSYCHOLOGY

Genetics

Genes are the blueprints that determine how we are going to be put together. As soon as you were conceived, your genetic makeup had predetermined what color hair you would have, how big your nose would be, and, to a large extent, how intelligent you would be. Genetics are important in psychology because they help explain how we got to be who we are.

Hormones

Hormones are chemicals secreted by our glands. These chemicals help regulate what is going on in the body. For example, the pituitary gland secretes a chemical that triggers growth in the body. The adrenal gland secretes a chemical that gives a burst of energy to help in dangerous situations.

Nervous System

The nervous system is made up of the parts of the body that allow us to think, act, and interact with the outside world. The nervous system is divided into two parts. First, the **central nervous system** is made up of the brain and spinal cord. Think of it as the control center. The second part is the **peripheral nervous system,** which is made up of all the other neurons that radiate to the rest of the body. These neurons serve as messengers, sending messages from the central nervous system to hands, feet, face, or whatever, and bringing messages to the central nervous system from the sense organs (eyes, ears, etc).

The central nervous system might send a message through the peripheral nervous system that says, "Tell the hand to wiggle the fingers." The peripheral nervous system might send a message to the central nervous system that says, "Take a look at what the eyes are picking up."

The peripheral nervous system is broken down even further into two parts. The **somatic nervous system** controls muscle movement and sense organs. These are voluntary functions, which means the central nervous system has to tell the arm to move, or it will not. The second part is the **autonomic nervous system,** which controls the heart, lungs, and digestive organs. When you see *autonomic,* think of automatic. The autonomic nervous system works automatically. That is, the central nervous system does not have to send a message down saying, for example, "take another breath."

Neurons

The nervous system is built of tiny structures called neurons. The neurons are not connected to one another directly, but they send messages to one another by secreting chemicals called **neurotransmitters** across the spaces in between them, which are called **synapses.**

Sample Essay Question

The three major subdivisions of the brain are the hindbrain, the midbrain, and the forebrain. Describe the basic function of each of these subdivisions.

IMPORTANT CONCEPTS IN GENERAL EXPERIMENTAL PSYCHOLOGY

Behaviorism

Behaviorism is a whole school of thought in psychology. Behaviorists believe that all human behavior can be boiled down to a simple sequence: something happens in the environment, and we respond to it. The implication of this sequence is that behaviorists believe that there is no need to study what goes on in peoples' heads. Yes, people think, but there is no need to pay attention to thought, because all behavior can be explained by the simple sequence of "something happens to us (a **stimulus**), and we respond." Behaviorists do not use terms like "thinking," "consciousness," and "unconscious." They believe that psychology should only study behaviors that can be observed.

When you think of behaviorists (remember that they do not care that you are thinking!), you might picture very serious people in white lab coats. Behaviorism is often contrasted with cognitive psychology and humanism because these are quite different schools of thought in psychology. Cognitive psychologists study thinking, and humanists want to treat people as their friends, rather than as very large white mice, as an extreme behaviorist might. (Keep in mind that we are drawing these comparisons very broadly only to help you remember the major differences between the schools of thought.)

When you reach the section on personality, note that behaviorism could also be considered a theory of personality. Instructors often ask questions about the differences between behaviorism, humanism, and Freudian theory. Behaviorism is rarely covered in textbooks in the personality chapter because behaviorism states that studying personality is useless since it is not observable behavior.

Classical Conditioning

Classical conditioning is learning by association. When two things are paired repeatedly, we learn to associate the two as occurring together. If you use an electric can opener to open your dog's food each evening, your dog will eventually learn to associate the sound of the can opener with food. He has been classically conditioned to associate the can opener with eating.

Each of the four parts of classical conditioning has a name. The names are easy to confuse, and they make perfect multiple-choice questions. First, the **unconditioned** sequence: the unconditioned sequence is what your subject does naturally, without any learning taking place. Going back to the can opener example, if you offer your dog food, he will begin to salivate. There is no need to teach the dog this trick. If you want to confirm it, take a steak and hold it out to your dog. The food in this example is the **unconditioned stimulus** and the dog's response, to salivate, is the **unconditioned response.** It is *un*conditioned because you do not have to do anything to get the dog to behave that way.

The **conditioned** sequence is what you teach your subject that he would not do naturally. In the case of your dog, the **conditioned stimulus** is the sound of the can opener, and the **conditioned response** is that the dog begins to salivate when he hears the can opener, even if no food is around. A dog would not salivate at the sound of a can opener if you usually fed him dry food out of a bag. It is not a natural behavior; that is why it is *conditioned.*

Classical conditioning is a **behavioral** technique. Notice that there is no interest in what the dog thinks of the can opener. The interest is in the dog's behavior. Something happens in the environment (the sound of the can opener always precedes dinner time), and this event leads to a behavior (salivating at the sound of the can opener). A stimulus in the environment and a response to that stimulus from the subject is the core of behaviorism.

Operant Conditioning

Operant conditioning is a learning technique based on a simple premise: we repeat behaviors that have good results, and we do not repeat behaviors that have bad results. If you start to pet a cat and it scratches your hand badly, you will probably not pet the cat again. You have learned through operant conditioning. The idea is simple. It gets a little more complicated when you start talking about the different types of results that might influence your behavior. (Read on to **reinforcement** and you'll see what we mean.)

Operant conditioning is a **behavioral** learning technique, because it involves something that happens in the environment (a stimulus) and some observable behavior from the subject in response. The man who made operant conditioning famous is the behaviorist B. F. Skinner. Skinner believed that operant conditioning could be used to make the world a better place. Just reward everyone for desirable behavior and punish them for undesirable behavior, starting when they are little, and you have the perfect society. His critics wanted to know who decides what is desirable behavior, and they also did not think too highly of the idea of manipulating people to get them to do what you want.

Reinforcement and Punishment

Operant conditioning takes place through reward and punishment. When we are rewarded for a behavior, we are likely to repeat that behavior. When we are punished for a behavior, we are not likely to repeat that behavior. In psychological jargon, rewards are called **reinforcements,** while punishment is called... punishment.

There are two kinds of reinforcement: **positive reinforcement** and **negative reinforcement.** Positive reinforcement is when something good happens to you when you engage in some behavior. If you study hard for a test and get an A, the A is a positive reinforcement for studying hard. If you tell a joke and people laugh, the laughter is positive reinforcement for telling a joke. Something good happens when you do something, so you do it more often.

Negative reinforcement is a little trickier. *Do not* confuse negative reinforcement with punishment. You will be asked to distinguish between negative reinforcement and punishment on a test (guaranteed). Negative reinforcement happens when you are rewarded by having something bad stop happening to you. If you are trying to study and your little sister is being really loud in the next room, you yell "shut up," and she shuts up, you have just been given negative reinforcement for yelling "shut up." Something bad stops happening. Another example of negative reinforcement: you're watching a TV show that you love, but the reception on the TV is awful. You find that when you move near the TV and hold your left arm straight out, the reception gets much better. So you stand there with your left arm straight out for 30 minutes. You are getting negative reinforcement from the TV set for holding your arm out. The bad reception stops happening.

Finally, there is **punishment.** Punishment works just like you think it does. You do something, and something happens as a result that leads to a decrease in the likelihood of that behavior happening in the future. If you drink too much and get a terrible hangover, you have been punished for drinking too much. If you cannot wait for a slice of pizza to cool off and you take a bite, and it sticks to the roof of your mouth and burns a layer of skin off, you have been punished for not waiting for the pizza to cool off.

Notice that reinforcements and punishments do not have to be intentional. Getting twenty dollars for returning a lost wallet is a positive reinforcement, but so is getting a smile from someone you are interested in dating.

Sensation and Perception

It is important to know the difference between sensation and perception. **Sensation** is the process of taking in information from the outside world through our senses. When we take in sounds, for example, our ears are picking up vibrations in the air and turning them into messages that are sent through **neurons** to the brain. Once these messages get to the brain, perception takes place. **Perception** is making sense of, or interpreting, this sensory information. For example, your ears pick up a loud "tooting" sound and send this information to the brain (sensation). Your brain interprets the sound as a train whistle (perception).

Stimulus

A stimulus is anything in the world that you might notice and respond to. An injection in your arm is a stimulus, and you may respond by flinching or yelling, or by trying to be cool and not flinch or yell even though you really want to. Your stomach growling is a stimulus, and you might respond by eating.

Motivation

Motivation is exactly what you think it is. We are motivated to get what we want, whether it is food, sex, a new car, or whatever. Everything we do is the result of some motivation, or, in other words, some need or want.

Sample Essay Question

What are four cues that people use to perceive depth? Describe each one, and give a specific example.

IMPORTANT CONCEPTS IN COGNITIVE PSYCHOLOGY

Consciousness

Consciousness is the same as awareness. To say you have consciousness is to say that you are aware of what is around you, and you are aware that you are thinking, sensing, and breathing. Do not think of consciousness as the opposite of being asleep. The key is awareness. Psychologists would argue that a moose is awake but not conscious because it is not aware that it is alive and thinking.

Unconscious

The unconscious is the part of our mind that works outside of our awareness. The unconscious mind has thoughts, feelings, and motives of which we are totally unaware. Freud was the first psychologist to emphasize the importance of the unconscious mind.

Information Processing

This phrase has really come into fashion in cognitive psychology because of the popularity of computers. Just as a computer is an information processor, psychologists talk about humans as information processors. This concept ties together sensation, perception, consciousness, cognition, and memory. We take information from the outside world, interpret it, use it, and store it, and this whole process is referred to as information processing.

Schema

A schema is a general set of ideas about some concept. We use schemata (plural) to make sense out of incoming information. For example, if you had never seen or heard of baseball before, any particular baseball game you watch would not make any sense. You have a schema for baseball, a general set of ideas about what it is and how it is played. You use this schema to make sense of what those people are doing out on a lawn with sticks and balls and big leather mittens.

Sample Essay Question

Compare and contrast the stage theory of memory with the organizational view of memory.

IMPORTANT CONCEPTS IN DEVELOPMENTAL PSYCHOLOGY

Attachment

Attachment is the bond that develops between an infant and its primary caregiver (usually the mother). Mother becomes the center of the infant's life. This relationship is very crucial to the infant, and a poor attachment (which usually results if the mother is mean or neglectful) usually affects the person negatively in later life, especially in terms of their **social development.**

Cognitive Development

Cognitive development refers to the ways that our thinking process changes as we get older. The main psychologist in cognitive development is Piaget. Remember his name and get a firm grasp of his theory of cognitive development, which is covered at length in your text and is mapped in this book (see Chapter 5).

Social Development

Social development is the study of how we go from being infants with no knowledge of social skills to well-mannered, socially skilled individuals. Social development looks at how our attitudes change, how we interact with others, and how we think about others as we get older. Social development is a mixture of social psychology and developmental psychology.

Gender Differences

Obviously, gender differences are differences between males and females. But gender differences are only the differences that we learn from other people, not the inborn, genetic differences. The fact that, on average, males are physically stronger than females is a **sex difference,** not a gender difference. The fact that females often cross their legs at the knee, but a "manly" male would never be caught dead in such a pose, is a gender difference.

Nature vs. Nurture

Nature vs. nurture is an important concept in psychology. Take any characteristic of a person, let's say intelligence, for example. The question is, is intelligence something we are born with, or something that develops depending on how we are raised? Does it help for a child to watch *Sesame Street* or is his or her intelligence already present at birth? The "nature" argument says that intelligence is genetic, that we are born with it. The "nurture" argument says that it depends on our experiences after we are born.

How do you settle the argument? By finding identical twins who were separated at birth and raised apart from each other. Identical twins have exactly the same genes. If they are raised apart, then you can answer the nature vs. nurture dilemma. If identical twins raised apart tend to have very similar IQs, then intelligence must be genetic, because they have the same "nature" but different "nurture." If their IQs tend not to be similar, then upbringing must have more to do with intelligence than genes.

By the way, intelligence is primarily genetic. (Keep in mind that almost no trait is 100% nature or nurture.)

Sample Essay Question

What is "nature vs. nurture"? How do psychologists go about studying whether a given characteristic is more influenced by "nature" or by "nurture"?

IMPORTANT CONCEPTS IN PERSONALITY PSYCHOLOGY

Defense Mechanism

Freud developed the idea of defense mechanisms. They are strategies that people use to defend themselves from some anxiety-provoking experience. Often, these anxious experiences involve some threat to their self-image. There are several different defense mechanisms. For example, **compensation** involves getting good at something in order to compensate for shortcomings at something else. A person wants to go to medical school, but he learns in college that he just does not have the ability to make the necessary grades. His ego is hurt, so he spends more of his time on football and becomes a star on the team. He thinks to himself, "I may not be the best student in the world, but who cares? I'm a great football player." According to Freud, defense mechanisms are **unconscious** because we use them without knowing it.

Ego, Id, and Superego

These are the three major structures that make up our personality, according to Freud. The id is our base, primitive instincts. The id wants everything right now and does not care about what will happen later as a result. Mostly the id wants sex and violence. It is like a greedy little gremlin. When we are born, we are pure id. As adults, our ids are totally unconscious. We are not aware of our ids, but they still have an influence over what we do.

The superego is our conscience. It worries about being good and moral. The superego is in direct opposition to the id. The superego develops out of the teachings of our parents, who teach us to be "civilized."

The ego is the part of you that you think of as "you." It is our conscious thoughts and feelings, the part of us that we are directly aware of. The ego balances the greedy desires of the id with the morals of the superego. If your ego gives in to your id too much, you become an immature, greedy, mean person. But if your ego gives in to your superego too much, you become a tight, judgmental, boring, stuffy person. The trick is to balance the two, which results in a healthy personality, according to Freud.

The best way to understand the relationship among the three structures is to imagine that you are the ego, and you have a little devil (id) and a little angel (superego) sitting on your shoulders, whispering in your ears. The devil is telling you to ruthlessly grab what you want. The angel is telling you to go home and watch reruns of *Little House on the Prairie*.

Psychoanalytic Theory

Psychoanalytic theory is the name of the theory of personality that Freud developed. The three major points are:

1. *Childhood:* Our personalities are formed in early childhood. What happens to us then determines who we will be for the rest of our lives.
2. *Sex:* Most of our problems are rooted in guilt about sexual desires, especially those we had as small children.
3. *The Unconscious:* Most of our "hangups" are unconscious. That is, we are not aware of them and their effect on us. These hangups mostly consist of guilt and anxiety about sexual desires from our childhood.

Keep in mind that Freud's theory is also the basis for a school of thought on how to treat mental illness. Psychoanalysts use Freud's ideas as the framework for treating psychological disorders.

Humanism

Humanism is a school of psychology that says that people are basically good. It sprang up in the 1960s to oppose behaviorism, which says that people are basically whatever their environment makes them, and psychoanalytic theory (Freud's), which says that people are basically evil (since they are born as ids). Humanism stresses the importance of self-esteem, love, hope, and other things central to people's development. The two most famous humanists are Abraham Maslow (who developed the hierarchy of needs we talked about in the memory chapter) and Carl Rogers. One way to remember humanists is to picture 1960s hippies with tie-dyed shirts sitting around talking about love.

Keep in mind that humanism is not only a theory of personality; it is a theory on how to treat mental illness as well. Humanistic therapists believe in giving people support, encouragement, and empathy in order to help them with their problems.

Trait Theory

Trait theorists believe that our personalities are best described in terms of personality traits, such as "outgoing," "humorous," "agreeable," and "stubborn." These traits describe what a particular person is like, and traits are said to be stable across situations, which is to say that a shy person will be shy at a party as well as at a funeral.

Sample Essay Question

Are people basically good or basically evil? Answer this question from a psychoanalytic perspective, a humanistic perspective, and a behavioristic perspective.

IMPORTANT CONCEPTS IN SOCIAL PSYCHOLOGY

Attitude

An attitude means the same thing in psychology as it does in "real" life. Your attitude about something is how you feel about it, whether you like that thing or not. People have attitudes about everything, from minority groups to abortion to dishwashing detergents. The main areas that are studied in attitudes are how people form their attitudes and how to change people's attitudes.

Cognitive Dissonance

If a person believes in living a healthy lifestyle, eats right and exercises, but also smokes, the person will probably experience cognitive dissonance. Cognitive dissonance occurs when we do things that are inconsistent with each other. If we believe one thing (be healthy) and do something that contradicts the belief (smoke), we feel uneasy, and we have to figure out some way to get rid of the inconsistency, or we continue to feel uneasy. In the case of the smoking, the most direct way to get rid of the inconsistency is to quit smoking. But often we do not choose the most direct way; we choose the easiest way. For a health-conscious smoker, the easiest way is to **rationalize** smoking: "I smoke low-tar cigarettes, which are not that bad for me," or "My grandfather smoked till he was 96, and he was as healthy as Jack LaLane." The key to reducing cognitive dissonance is to make the inconsistency appear consistent in your mind. Then the uneasiness goes away, and you can puff your way to an early grave without any misgivings.

Norms

Norms are expectations we have within society or within some subgroup of society about how people should behave. Norms tell us what is normal behavior in a given situation and what is not. If you belong to a gang, the norms of the group are that you should be tough, loyal to the gang, and should wear a baseball cap all the time. If you are in a gang, and you help old people cross the street, you are violating the group's norms.

Social Cognition

Social cognition is a sub-discipline within social psychology. Social cognition looks at people's thoughts and beliefs about other people. It is a mixture of social psychology and cognitive psychology. Social cognition looks at how we form first impressions of others and why we form stereotypes, for example.

Social Comparison

Social comparison is our tendency to evaluate how we are doing by comparing ourselves to others. How do you know if you are a good tennis player? By playing against someone you consider good, and seeing how well you do. We engage in social comparison all the time. If you get a B on a test, and find out that 90% of the class got A's, you are disappointed in the grade. But if you find out that 90% of the class got D's, you are probably very happy with the grade.

Sample Essay Question

What can you do to increase the possibility that a person will like you?

IMPORTANT CONCEPTS IN CLINICAL PSYCHOLOGY

Anxiety Disorders

Anxiety disorders are mental disorders that revolve around some sort of fear or anxiety. **Phobias** are anxiety disorders. A phobia is a fear of some object or event, such as fear of heights. **Panic attacks,** where a person suddenly becomes absolutely terrified for no apparent reason, are another type of anxiety disorder.

Dissociative Disorders

The best way to describe dissociative disorders is to say that the sufferer has "split" in some manner. In the case of amnesia, a person's memory, or some part of it, has split off. People with **amnesia** cannot remember some portion of their past. Another dissociative disorder is **multiple personality disorder.** A person with multiple personality disorder can be thought of as two or more people living inside one body. In this case, the person's personality has "split" into a number of different thinking, feeling entities.

Mood Disorders

Mood disorders are problems that people have with their moods. The two main ones are depression and manic-depression. You know what **depression** is, but be sure you know the symptoms and causes. **Manic-depression** (or **bipolar disorder**) is similar to depression, but instead of being in the pits of despair for weeks or months straight, a manic-depressive will be in the pits of despair for a while, then on top of the world or agitated for a while, and then back to despair, like an emotional roller coaster.

Neurotic vs. Psychotic Disorders

These are general ways of describing all mental disorders. Neurotic means "the disorder is not *too* serious," while psychotic means "the disorder is serious." A neurotic disorder is one that is disturbing to the person who has it, but the person usually can keep a job, have friends, and basically lead a normal life. For instance, anxiety disorders tend to be neurotic. A person with a psychotic disorder is extremely disturbed and usually has to be hospitalized. **Schizophrenia** is a psychotic disorder.

Schizophrenia

Schizophrenia is a mental illness that involves losing touch with reality. A person with schizophrenia thinks in bizarre ways, hears voices, and generally acts very strangely. Most people we think of as being "crazy" are usually suffering from schizophrenia. *Do not* confuse schizophrenia with multiple personality disorder. Multiple personality falls under the heading of **dissociative disorders** and is totally different from schizophrenia.

Behavior Modification

Behavior modification is a behavioristic technique for treating mental illness. You try to cure the mental illness by changing the behaviors, or symptoms, of the mental illness. No attempt is made to discover what is causing those symptoms, because that would involve dealing with the sufferer's thoughts. Behavior modification works well with some disorders, but not as well with others. If you are trying to cure alcoholism, for example, you might punish the alcoholic each time he or she takes a drink. According to the notion of **operant conditioning,** a behavior that results in punishment is less likely to be repeated, so eventually the alcoholic should stop drinking. Notice that no attempt is made to find out *why* the person became an alcoholic. The focus is on changing the behavior of drinking.

Psychotherapy

Psychotherapy is the general term used to describe the various treatments of mental illness that involve talking to the troubled person. A psychotherapist might be a **humanistic** psychotherapist, a **behavioral** psychotherapist, or a **psychoanalyst** or might be eclectic (using a number of different approaches, and seeing what works in a given situation). There are literally hundreds of different schools of psychotherapy that are practiced.

Sample Essay Question

What are the symptoms of depression, and how is it treated?

PSYCHOLOGICAL CONCEPTS RELATED TO RESEARCH METHODS

Correlation

If a correlation exists between two events, it means that the events are related to one another. Intelligence and grade point average are correlated. The thing about correlation is that it does not say anything about the cause and the effect. It simply says that when one thing happens, the other thing usually happens as well. For example, there is a correlation between being happy and being outgoing. People who are outgoing are happier than people who are shy. Does this mean you should be more outgoing if you want to be happier? Maybe, maybe not. It could be that being happy causes people to be more outgoing. Aren't you more sociable when you are happy? Or it could be that something else makes people both happier and more outgoing. Maybe people who get lots of calcium in their diet are happier and more outgoing, who knows? A correlation means that two things are related, but it does not imply anything about what causes what. In psychological jargon, we say that "correlation does not imply causation."

Experiment

An experiment is the only way to find out with any confidence if something causes something else to happen (compare to **correlation**). By using a particular set of rules about how to set things up, a researcher eliminates other possible explanations and can say with some confidence that something is the cause (or **independent variable**) and something is the effect (or **dependent variable**).

Dependent Variable

In an experiment, the dependent variable is the effect. The experimenter is trying to figure out how the dependent variable can be controlled, or manipulated. If you run an experiment to see if punishing a rat for making mistakes while running a maze will make it do better, the dependent variable is how well the rat runs the maze. The rat's performance in the maze is what you are trying to control or manipulate through punishment; the rat's performance is the effect.

Another way to think of the dependent variable is as the subject's response to what you do to him, her, or it. If you punish the rat, how does it respond in the maze? The response is the dependent variable.

Independent Variable

In an experiment, the independent variable is the cause. The researcher is trying to show that you can use the independent variable to get a particular effect. If you run an experiment to see if punishing a rat for making mistakes while running a maze will make it do better, the punishment is the independent variable. The researcher is trying to see if punishment causes improved performance in the maze.

APPENDIX 2

SAMPLE INTRODUCTORY PSYCHOLOGY TEST

Below you will find 30 multiple choice questions. The answers, with explanations, are found at the end of the sample test.

1. Seeing is to light as smell is to

   a. chemicals.
   b. taste.
   c. vibrations.
   d. light.
   e. pressure.

2. If a researcher studies group decision-making, he or she is conducting research in which general area of psychology?

   a. Biological
   b. Clinical
   c. Social
   d. Developmental
   e. Personality

3. How many items of information can you hold in short-term memory at one time?

   a. About 3
   b. About 7
   c. About 15
   d. About 100
   e. An unlimited amount

4. How many stages of REM sleep does the average person go through in 8 hours of sleep?

   a. 1
   b. 2
   c. 3–5
   d. 6–10
   e. 11–15

5. Psychoanalysis is most closely associated with

   a. behaviorism.
   b. Maslow.
   c. cognitive dissonance.
   d. memory.
   e. id, ego, and superego.

6. Which of the following is considered an anxiety disorder?

   a. Schizophrenia
   b. Depression
   c. Multiple personality disorder
   d. Phobia
   e. Antisocial personality disorder

7. Which concept was developed by a prominent humanistic psychologist?

   a. Id
   b. Operant conditioning
   c. Self-actualization
   d. Extroversion
   e. Collective unconscious

8. Kohlberg's first level of moral development, which comprises stage 1 and stage 2, is morality based on

   a. logic.
   b. shame and guilt.
   c. the letter of the law.
   d. self-interest.
   e. religious beliefs.

9. Which researcher was concerned with cognitive development?

   a. Kohlberg
   b. Piaget
   c. Erikson
   d. Maslow
   e. Freud

10. Classic and operant conditioning are part of a school of thought in psychology that is called

    a. humanism.
    b. psychoanalytic.
    c. functionalism.
    d. cognitive.
    e. behaviorism.

11. Identical twins reared apart are extremely useful in studying which basic question in development?

    a. Are there "critical periods" in development?
    b. Are there really stages in moral development?
    c. Which is more influential in development: nature or nurture?
    d. Both a and b
    e. Both b and c

12. Which is NOT a primary motive or "drive"?

    a. Need for love
    b. Need for sleep
    c. Need for food
    d. Need for sex
    e. Need to avoid pain

13. You see something on the ground that you think is a dime. It is not really a dime; it is a pop-top from a soda can, but you do not notice this. Which of the following is true?

    a. You sensed a dime on the ground.
    b. You perceived a dime on the ground.
    c. You perceived a pop-top from a soda can on the ground.
    d. You neither sensed nor perceived a pop-top on the ground.
    e. both a and b

14. The function of the corpus callosum is to

    a. control muscle movement in the body.
    b. allow the left hemisphere of the brain to control the right side of the body and the right hemisphere to control the left side of the body.
    c. pass information between the somatic nervous system and the autonomic nervous system.
    d. pass information between the left and right hemispheres of the brain.
    e. connect the brain to the sensory organs.

15. In what lobe of the brain will you find the sensory cortex?

    a. Frontal
    b. Lateral
    c. Parietal
    d. Temporal
    e. Occipital

16. What are phonemes?

    a. The smallest units of speech in a language that have meaning
    b. Chemicals that animals emit into the air to attract mates
    c. The smallest units of speech in a language that have a distinctive sound
    d. The rules that determine the order in which words are put together in a sentence

17. Psychology developed out of which two disciplines?

    a. Sociology and biology
    b. Philosophy and sociology
    c. Physics and political science
    d. Biology and philosophy
    e. Sociology and chemistry

18. Which of the following groups of drugs contains only drugs that are not physically addictive?

    a. Alcohol, nicotine, caffeine
    b. Marijuana, LSD, cocaine
    c. Heroin, valium, cocaine
    d. Caffeine, LSD, valium
    e. Opium, heroin, valium

19. When an intoxicated person staggers, it is because the alcohol has affected his or her

    a. cerebral cortex.
    b. cerebellum.
    c. limbic system.
    d. mid-brain.
    e. reticular formation.

20. After conditioning has occurred, if the unconditioned stimulus is no longer presented after the conditioned stimulus, then _____ will occur.

    a. discrimination
    b. generalization
    c. conditioned inhibition
    d. extinction
    e. punishment

21. Johnny gets bitten by a dog while eating a cherry lollipop. Now he gets anxious whenever he tastes or smells a cherry lollipop. In this example, the conditioned stimulus is

    a. the lollipop.
    b. anxiety.
    c. the dog bite.
    d. running away from the dog.
    e. Johnny.

22. Fear of snakes is called

    a. hematophobia.
    b. ophidiophobia.
    c. acrophobia.
    d. claustrophobia.
    e. agoraphobia.

23. Which of the following is NOT a common characteristic of self-actualized people?

    a. They tend to lead simple, spontaneous lives.
    b. They tend to have a good sense of humor.
    c. They tend to have a strong drive to achieve honors and recognition.
    d. They tend to develop a few very close friendships.
    e. They tend to have more peak experiences than other people.

24. Which of the following is true about depression?

    a. It is more common in females.
    b. It usually does not go away without medication or psychological treatment.
    c. Depression is not related to stressful life events.
    d. Once a depressed person gets better, he or she is unlikely to get depressed again.
    e. None of the above.

25. The main point of the "bridge study," where male students were stopped by a female interviewer on a high, swinging bridge was

    a. Physical attraction is a powerful motivator and can cancel out other motivators such as fear of heights.
    b. The fear associated with heights can squash other motivations, even those as powerful as sexual attraction.
    c. It is possible to mistake one emotion for another, such as confusing the fear of heights with sexual attraction.
    d. Males are more driven by sexual motivations, while females are more motivated by survival motives.
    e. All of the above.

26. The presence of other people _____ our performance on simple, well learned tasks and _____ our performance on difficult, unfamiliar tasks.

    a. improves; improves
    b. hinders; hinders
    c. improves; hinders
    d. hinders; improves
    e. has no effect on; hinders

27. Words studied underwater are later better recalled underwater; words studied on land are better recalled on land. This finding best illustrates the importance of

    a. the primacy/recency effect.
    b. rehearsal.
    c. automatic processing.
    d. active processing.
    e. state-dependent memory.

28. Which theory of emotion states that emotions result from the interpretation of physiological arousal?

    a. Cannon-Bard theory
    b. Adaptation level theory
    c. Opponent-process theory
    d. James-Lange theory
    e. Schachter's two-factor theory

29. Discovering a general truth from specific instances is called
    a. a hypothesis.
    b. deductive reasoning.
    c. the confirmation bias.
    d. inductive reasoning.
    e. the availability heuristic.

30. Remembering how to ride a bicycle is an example of
    a. procedural memory.
    b. short-term memory.
    c. declarative memory.
    d. eidetic imagery.
    e. semantic encoding.

ANSWERS

1. The correct answer is a: Sight involves sensing light waves, while smelling involves sensing chemicals in the air.

2. The correct answer is c: Any time research involves interactions among people—like group decision-making—the research is in social psychology.

3. The correct answer is c: Seven plus or minus two items.

4. The correct answer is c: Each "cycle" of sleep takes about 1 1/2 to 2 hours. Because we dream once per cycle, we dream 3 to 5 times per night.

5. The correct answer is e: Psychoanalysis is Freud's method of doing psychotherapy. The id, ego, and superego are also Freudian terms, while the other terms listed are not Freudian.

6. The correct answer is d.

7. The correct answer is c: Maslow developed the concept of self-actualization.

8. The correct answer is d: The first (lowest) level of moral development involves deciding whether something is right or wrong based on what consequences (reward or punishment) it might have for the individual.

9. The correct answer is b.

10. The correct answer is e.

11. The correct answer is c. Be careful not to be misled when you see choices like d and e. It is tempting to conclude that your professor would not have put that type of choice there unless one of them is correct. Your professor may put them there because he or she could not think of any other responses or because students do find them so tempting!

12. The correct answer is a. Love is not one of our primary motives, which are also known as instinctual drives.

13. The correct answer is b. Remember, sensing is what your senses do; they take in what is in the outside world and send it to the brain to be interpreted. The brain perceives (or interprets) the sensations. You interpreted what was on the ground to be a dime, so you perceived a dime. You sensed a pop-top from a coke can; a pop-top was on the ground, so that is what your senses picked up. Your brain made the mistake, not your eyes.

14. The correct answer is d.

15. The correct answer is c.

16. The correct answer is c.

17. The correct answer is d.

18. The correct answer is b. A physically addictive drug is one that can lead to physical withdrawal symptoms if a person takes it regularly and then stops all at once.

19. The correct answer is b. The cerebellum controls balance and coordination—remember "Sara-bell"?

20. The correct answer is d. Extinction is when we "unlearn" an association because it stops happening. If Pavlov keeps ringing the bell and food is not showing up, the dogs will eventually stop salivating when they hear the bell.

21. The correct answer is a. The conditioned stimulus is the occurrence that would not naturally lead to the response that occurs. A cherry lollipop would not naturally lead to anxiety, so it is a conditioned stimulus.

22. The correct answer is b. Remember the image of the snake biting its own tail to form an "O," the first letter in ophidiophobia.

23. The correct answer is c. According to Maslow, self-actualized people are not interested in personal glory; they are interested in the good of people.

24. The correct answer is a.

25. The correct answer is c. It is not uncommon for a professor to ask about specific experiments in psychology, as we noted in Chapter 2.

26. The correct answer is c. This phenomenon is known as social facilitation.

27. The correct answer is e. Recall our discussion of studying in your pajamas in Chapter 6.

28. The correct answer is e.

29. The correct answer is d.

30. The correct answer is a. Procedural memory is our memory for how to do things (procedures). Declarative memory is our memory for specific facts, such as our phone number or what we had for breakfast.

INDEX